PUBLICATIONS OF THE
MINNESOTA HISTORICAL SOCIETY

Rainy River Country

*A Brief History
of the Region Bordering
Minnesota
and Ontario
by*
GRACE LEE NUTE

THE MINNESOTA HISTORICAL SOCIETY
St. Paul, 1950

LIBRARY OF CONGRESS CATALOG CARD NUMBER: 71-96385
STANDARD BOOK NUMBER: 87351-008-9

Foreword

IN 1941 THE *Minnesota Historical Society published Grace Lee Nute's* The Voyageur's Highway, *a history of the border-lake country of Minnesota and Ontario eastward from Rainy Lake. The little book has had so wide an appeal that it is now in its fifth printing.* Rainy River Country *may be regarded as a companion volume to* The Voyageur's Highway, *for it tells the story of the border country to the west — the region of the Rainy River and the two lakes that it joins, Rainy Lake and Lake of the Woods.*

The book is based on Dr. Nute's broad and thorough knowledge of the source materials relating to the Rainy River country. It is accurate history, and it is written with simplicity and charm. The author's familiarity with the area and its long history, her affection for it, and her sensitiveness to its beauty bring warmth and life to her narrative.

Rainy River Country *tells of the earliest people who passed through the region, Mongoloid men from Asia; of the mound builders who followed them; and of the Sioux Indians and, later, the Chippewa, who lived on or near the river, fishing, gathering wild rice, and hunting the elk, moose, bear, caribou, and the smaller animals that roamed the valley. It reveals how traders traveled up and down the river for two centuries in quest of fortunes in furs and skins; how lighthearted voyageurs, singing their chansons, canoed over the waterway and toiled across portages with their heavy loads; and how missionaries came to heal the souls of dwellers in the wilderness. It tells of explorers who passed that way in search of the*

Foreword

Western Sea or of routes to the Arctic; of settlers who traveled the river on their way to new homes in the West; of prospectors seeking gold; and of artists recording the face of the country in their sketchbooks. And it relates how farms were opened; how towns and villages grew up; how lumbering activities were carried on; how great industries developed; and how tourists have come in increasing numbers to that magnificent vacation land shared by the people of Minnesota and Ontario as a single, friendly community.

The publication of Rainy River Country *has been made possible by a generous gift to the Society from the Minnesota and Ontario Paper Company. The Society is deeply grateful to the Company, and to its public-spirited president, Mr. Donald D. Davis, for his interest in the book from the time of its inception.*

HAROLD DEAN CATER

MINNESOTA HISTORICAL SOCIETY
ST. PAUL, 1950

Acknowledgments

AT THIS TIME I take pleasure in saying "Thank you" to the following persons and institutions that have helped me in the preparation of this book: Paul Kinports of the Minnesota and Ontario Paper Company, International Falls; Paul Anderson, editor of the International Falls Daily Journal; Lucile Kane, curator of manuscripts, and others of the staff of the Minnesota Historical Society; Ernest Oberholtzer of Ranier; the Hudson's Bay Company and Clifford Wilson of Winnipeg, the editor of the company's magazine, The Beaver; Robert Fritz of International Falls; Frank Brooks Hubachek of Chicago; Frank Gillmor of Ironwood, Michigan; the staffs of the Hibbing Public Library and the Duluth Public Library; the Oliver Iron Mining Company; the Tourist Bureau at Kenora, Ontario; various officials and staff members of the Minnesota and Ontario Paper Company and its subsidiaries; and John Dobie of the Minnesota Department of Conservation.

GRACE LEE NUTE

MINNESOTA HISTORICAL SOCIETY
ST. PAUL, 1950

Contents

Illustrations

Illustrations

xii

Illustrations

Fleurs de Lys

DEEP IN the midland of North America, John McKay stepped from his York boat one summer day in 1793, after rowing up the eighty-five-mile course of the stately Rainy River from Lake of the Woods to a thundering cataract at the outlet of Rainy Lake. A few days later, having determined upon a site for the first Hudson's Bay Company trading post in that section of the country, he began to build his fort and to keep the diary required of all "servants" of the venerable company. "This is one of the Beautifullest rivers I ever saw in this country," he penned in his inimitable style, anticipating the verdict of scores of other Scotch and English traders and travelers. That same year, for example, a North West Company clerk, John Macdonell, wrote in his diary, "This is deemed the most beautiful River in the N.W." A few years later Sir Alexander Mackenzie expressed his sentiment: "This is one of the finest rivers in the North-West." Many others wrote in similar admiration.

McKay and his company were late comers in the area. More than sixty years earlier there had been a French post close to the site on which McKay built; the remains were still visible in his day. The North West Company also had moved in long before his arrival, had built a post, and was entrenched there so strongly that the Hudson's Bay Company post could not compete profitably, and it was abandoned before 1800, not to reappear until 1816.

Not even the French were the earliest human beings to appropriate the region. Before them the Sioux Indians had lived throughout the basin of the Rainy River and about the two lakes that it joined. Chippewa Indians moved in shortly after the French appeared, and the ensuing strife between the two groups of aborigines was fearful. When the French likewise were driven out by invaders — by the British in 1763 — it was clear that the Chippewa, or Ojibway, as they are frequently termed, were the forest dwellers who would do business with the new white conquerors.

Even the Sioux were not the first men and women to live on the river and about the lakes. As they speared or netted great sturgeons and whitefish in the river and at the falls, they must have glimpsed high mounds of earth, obviously made by man, under the tall hardwood trees that lined the banks. Later, as they stalked the wary moose, caribou, elk, bear, or lynx alongshore, they doubtless stopped to investigate those burial mounds, in which their ancestors, or at least some earlier people, had interred their dead. They could not fail to find some of the artifacts placed with the corpses — arrowheads and spearheads, fishing equipment, women's tools for preparing skins, and other items. Some of them are so primitive that even a Sioux Indian would have believed them old-fashioned; but some are so cleverly wrought of copper that all who have seen them are amazed.

Neither Sioux nor Chippewa know much about these mound builders, but it is now believed that the first Asiatics to find a route through the continent, on their way to people North and South America, passed this way; that their descendants, shortly after the great ice sheet began to retreat, settled here and built up a highly interesting civilization of their own. For tools and weapons have been found with such geological or other accompanying evidence as to convince scholars that man was in the region at least ten thousand years ago. Whether

INDIAN MOUND AT LAUREL

[From a photograph owned by Paul Anderson.]

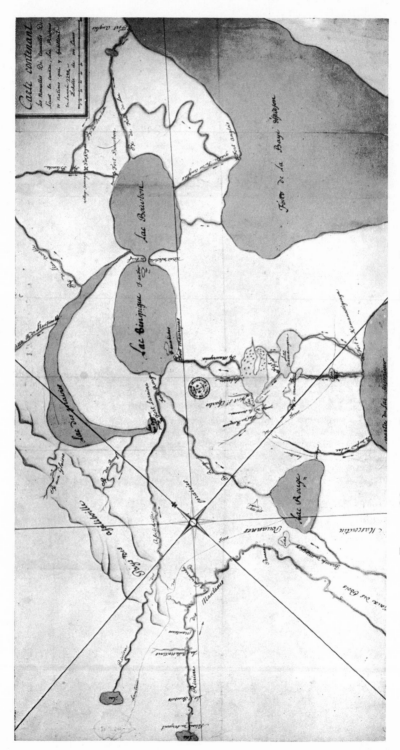

FRENCH MAP OF 1740 SHOWING THE RAINY RIVER COUNTRY

[From a photograph of the original in the Library of the Hydrographic Service of the Marine, Paris.]

or not the mound builders were direct ancestors of the Sioux is not proved, but the general consensus of opinion points in that direction.

When the first human beings arrived, they doubtless found a broad, milky-white lake spread over much of what is now the Rainy River basin. After aeons of geological turbulence — for this is one of the most ancient bits of our earth — a great, white stillness fell. Glaciers, in the form of slowly moving rivers of snow ice, ground inexorably over this region from the northeast and the northwest; their pathways crossed in the valley of the Little Fork River, a southern tributary of Rainy River. The ice rivers as they melted left characteristic debris and soil behind: gray from the northwest, red from the northeast.

Above the greenstone, from two to three billion years old — oldest of earth's known outcropping rocks; above the old granites, ejected from the core of the earth over a billion years ago; above the so-called "younger" granites, probably five hundred million years "young"; above the iron formations, laid down about half a billion years ago; and even above the limestones that covered this and much of the continent some hundred million years ago — above these successive layers of the massive crust of this planet, the glaciers melted and left behind them an inland, unsalted sea. It spread out over the land from Rainy Lake and Vermilion Lake on the east to the Red River Valley and beyond on the west; and from far up in Canada on the north to the head of the Minnesota River on the south. The first human beings of the area doubtless hunted the mastodon and other prehistoric animals about the edges of this extensive lake, which slowly vanished, leaving excellent soil as its legacy. Artifacts of live ivory have been found on the beaches of this Glacial Lake Agassiz, to give it

3

its modern name. They show that men hunted now extinct creatures there at the time of the melting of the ice.

When Jacques de Noyons, and perhaps other Frenchmen, arrived in 1688 or thereabout, a vast forest covered most of the Rainy River basin, with hundreds of lakes and many muskegs interspersed. It was truly a lush wilderness, rich in trees, flowers, birds, mammals, fishes, and insects. Most important, as far as white men were concerned, it could be reached with relative ease. For Rainy River was to become the important link in the chain of lakes and streams that stretched from the Gulf of St. Lawrence on the east to the Columbia River on the west. Traders might go by a variety of routes to the Ohio, the Missouri, or the Mississippi; but to reach the great storehouse of beaver and other important pelts, they must pass this way, since the finest skins were most numerous north and northwest of Lake Superior. It is true that the Hudson's Bay Company might have sent its traders with even greater ease to that storehouse, for the corporation had posts on Hudson Bay, the eastern gateway to the region, after 1668; but the fact remains that the company did not send its traders inland up the Churchill, Nelson, and Saskatchewan rivers until it was compelled to meet the rivalry of its powerful competitor of the Rainy River route, the North West Company, in the 1770's. Prior to that time the Londoners neither used the great western rivers tributary to Hudson Bay nor allowed the French, who were excluded by the Treaty of Utrecht in 1713, to do so.

The man chosen to reopen De Noyons' old route and build a fort near his wintering post in 1731 was Pierre Gaultier, sieur de la Vérendrye. Of the third generation of a well-known Three Rivers family interested in western exploration, La Vérendrye was the son of a governor of Three Rivers and the grandson of Pierre Boucher, who, in 1664, published the first history of New France. In his book Boucher mentioned a great lake in the West, in which there was an island containing copper — obviously a reference to Lake Superior. The grandson, born in New France, entered the army in 1697 at the age of twelve years, served in the New England campaigns of Queen Anne's War, crossed to France and took part in the campaigns against the Duke of Marlborough, and was wounded nine times by saber and bullet in the decisive battle of the war, Malplaquet. Later, on Lake of the Woods, those old wounds bothered him.

Ever a will-o'-the-wisp, luring many a great man on to danger and famous exploit, the idea of a Northwest Passage teased La Vérendrye at his fur-trading post on Lake Nipigon in 1727 and 1728 until he inquired of his native customers about the vast hinterland that stretched north and west from his post. One of them, Auchagah, told him of water to the west that was ill tasting and that moved back and forth. Thinking ever of the Western Sea, La Vérendrye snatched at the idea presented by Auchagah, concluded that the description fitted salt water and tides, and got the Indian to draw a map of the West on a piece of birchbark. This La Vérendrye sent to Charles Beauharnois, governor of New France, with a request to be allowed to search for the Northwest Passage revealed, so he believed, by the map. The governor referred his request to the king of France, who finally authorized the expedition but refused financial assistance. A monopoly of the fur trade in new areas, however, was permitted the explorer.

Copies of Auchagah's map were made at once in France, where they have remained and are still to be seen. They show the river and lake communications between Lake Superior and Lake of the Woods, including the one by way of Pigeon

River, the Kaministiquia River route, and a part of the St. Louis River trail to Vermilion River. The great carrying place around the rapids of the Pigeon River is named "the Grand Portage" on this map; Rainy Lake is called "Tecamamiouen," a Monsoni word describing the rain-like mist that rose from the falls; Lake of the Woods is "Lac des Bois"; and the Sioux are shown around both lakes, the Cree north of Lake of the Woods, and the Monsoni north of Rainy Lake. This is the first known map of any detail showing the region between Lake Superior and Lake of the Woods, and it is surprisingly accurate. Even Lake Saganaga is shown and named. Out of Lake of the Woods flows a river marked "to the River of the West." From later reports we know that this was the Winnipeg River connecting with the Saskatchewan by way of Lake Winnipeg. Just as the Indians intimated, one could reach the Western Sea by this route, but La Vérendrye ignored the time element involved.

Following Auchagah's map, La Vérendrye and three of his four stalwart sons left New France in 1731 and reached the Grand Portage later that summer. With them went about fifty soldiers and voyageurs, or canoemen, besides Charles Dufrost, sieur de la Jémeraye, La Vérendrye's nephew, who already had had experience in the West and was a capable leader of men. When a sort of mutiny occurred at the Grand Portage among the soldiers and voyageurs, it was La Jémeraye who, with a canoeful of men, went on, map in hand, while La Vérendrye stayed with the remainder of the force at the mouth of the Kaministiquia River. There, where a French post had been established in 1717 near or on the site of Duluth's post of the 1680's, the leader spent the winter.

La Jémeraye built his wintering post at the outlet of Lac La Pluie, or Rainy Lake, and called it "Fort St. Pierre" in honor

6

of his uncle, who, with the rest of the men, joined him there in 1732. From the voluminous letters, reports, and diaries kept by the Vérendryes, we know that Fort St. Pierre stood on the north bank of the river, on Pither's Point of today, about two miles east of Fort Frances, where one of two rapids above the falls impeded navigation. It was a timber structure, having two opposing gates and two bastions. There were two main buildings inside the fifty-pace stockade, each of which had two rooms heated by a double fireplace. A seven-foot *chemin de ronde* and a double row of pickets, thirteen feet above ground, surrounded the buildings. There was a storeroom in one of the bastions, and a powder magazine was, as in all forts of the day, an essential but dangerous part of the establishment.

This was the first of seven posts established by La Vérendrye on the water communications revealed to him by Auchagah. It was the most strategic of them all, it would seem; for, during the next century and a half and indeed even longer, there was hardly a year in which some post did not occupy the site of this fort or some place in the immediate vicinity. Finally, one post of the Hudson's Bay Company was given the name "Fort Frances" in 1830, and little by little it grew into a hamlet, a village, and at last a city of the same name.

The second post erected by La Vérendrye was on a small island close to the mainland on the west shore of Lake of the Woods. It was built in 1732 and was called "Fort St. Charles," perhaps in triple honor of Charles de la Jémeraye, Governor Charles Beauharnois, and the Jesuit missionary, Charles Michel Mesaiger, who joined the first La Vérendrye expedition at Michilimakinac in 1731. Because its ruins may still be seen and because more was written of it by La Vérendrye and his men than about Fort St. Pierre, we are able to visualize it more clearly. It extended about sixty feet along Angle River and about a hundred feet southward into the forest. Consisting of four main buildings with fireplaces, a powder magazine, a storehouse, a watchtower, and a stone, or partially stone, chapel, it was a little smaller than Fort Beauharnois on Lake Pepin, and somewhat larger than Fort St. Pierre, which it superseded for some years, at least, as headquarters for La Vérendrye. Yet it was not a very substantial affair, if we are to believe a man who lived there and who described it as "but an enclosure," inside which were "a few huts of squared logs, calked with earth and covered with bark."

Preserved in Canada to this day are lists of *congés*, or licenses to trade, issued yearly to merchants of New France, which give the names of men who went to Fort St. Charles or passed through it to other western posts as long as France retained the northern part of the continent. From La Vérendrye's letters, reports, maps, and other papers, which have been published in recent years, we know much of what went on at Fort St. Charles during his lifetime, that is, until the end of 1749. They give the minutiae of a life that consisted of elemental things — building shelters, hunting, fishing, getting acquainted with Indians and native ways, and exploring the surrounding country. To learn about the region and ways to the Western Sea, La Vérendrye held many councils with the Indians. In a large gathering during the winter of 1733–34, he inquired about the mineral resources of the area and was told of several places just beyond Lake Superior where iron could be found. This is perhaps the earliest record of iron in a region that later supplied nearly three-fourths of the nation's annual output of that ore, and about a third of the world's output.

The wild rice, the fish, and the moose, caribou, and other game of the region, as well as great flocks of migrating or nest-

8

ing wild fowl, supplied the newcomers with the necessities of life, just as for centuries they had been drawn upon by the mound builders and other, later, aborigines of this region. As many as four thousand whitefish, not to mention trout, sturgeon, and other kinds, were caught one autumn. There was even a little fort garden, in which corn, peas, and other cultivated vegetables were grown. Forest fires were destructive and hazardous then as now. The second of three Jesuit priests to serve as a missionary at Fort St. Charles, Father Jean Pierre Aulneau, wrote to his relatives in France that in 1735 he "journeyed nearly all the way" from Lake Superior to Lake of the Woods "through fire and a thick, stifling smoke," which prevented him from "even once catching a glimpse of the sun."

The young priest's stay was brief. In June, 1736, he started back with twenty or so men, including the eldest son of La Vérendrye, to meet and speed on a flotilla of canoes bringing much-needed food and other supplies from Canada. Before meeting the inward-bound men, the departing group encountered a war party of Sioux on an island in Lake of the Woods. Because all the Frenchmen were killed, the true facts of the massacre have never been obtained. The stories told by René Bourassa, who either accompanied the group or was close at hand, vary so greatly that the facts cannot now be ascertained. Even the site of the mass murder is in question, for Massacre Island, where a monument was erected in 1890, may or may not be the true location. Skeletons and skulls of the victims were taken up by La Vérendrye and buried in Fort St. Charles. There they were found and identified in 1908.

Another tragedy came to the leader that same year of 1736. La Vérendrye's nephew, the Sieur de la Jémeraye, died and was buried in the wilderness, probably at the mouth of Roseau River, which long served both Indians and traders as the connecting link between the navigation of Lake of the Woods and that of the Red River of the North. Indeed, La Vérendrye's lot was most difficult in those years. Suspected of graft and greed, he was even removed from leadership at one time, and he had to make many journeys to Canada to keep old support and gain new. This was an unsavory period in Canadian political history, one which explains in some measure why France lost her great colony in 1763.

Probably there were minor posts besides the two on Rainy Lake and Lake of the Woods. Bourassa seems to have built a temporary substitute for Fort St. Pierre in 1736 at the mouth of the Vermilion River, on or near Crane Lake. Recently the remains of a fort have been found on the northwest side of that lake, just about on the site of a French post shown on a manuscript map of 1740, now in French archives. The remains of another French post were found in 1792 in the English River country, north of Rainy River, by James Sutherland, a Hudson's Bay Company man. This old fort was erected on one of the "back roads" from Rainy Lake to the Winnipeg River by a French trader named Burdigno, according to an old Indian woman at Grand Portage in the 1790's, who remembered it as having been built about sixty years earlier. It was on Ball Lake, near Sutherland's Escabitchewan House. Probably there were still other posts.

La Vérendrye's chief disappointment was that, despite all his efforts and journeys, he did not find the Sea of the West. One of his expeditions got to the "Shining Mountains," long identified as the Rocky Mountains, but now thought to have been the Black Hills of South Dakota; for one of the expedition's lead plates, inscribed and dated, was found near Pierre, South Dakota, in 1913. Nevertheless, from Fort St. Pierre, Fort St. Charles, and other posts to the west, La Vérendrye garnered data and information on a vast area across the continent, and thus aided materially in making that section of North America much better known. He was relieved of his leadership in 1744, when Nicolas Joseph de Noyelles succeeded him, but he was reinstated later, and he even won promotion to a

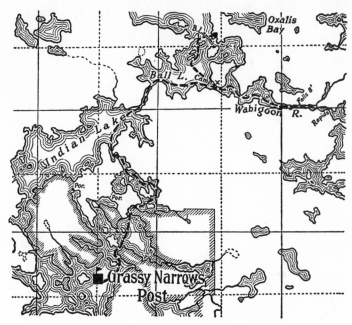

BALL LAKE, SITE OF BURDIGNO'S POST
[From *The Beaver*, March, 1949]

captaincy in 1746 and the coveted Cross of St. Louis in 1749. While making plans to return to his post the next year, he died in Canada on December 6, 1749. His place as commandant of the Posts of the Sea of the West was taken by Jacques Legardeur, sieur de St. Pierre, who arrived in the West in 1750 and remained until he was superseded by Louis Francois de la Corne in 1753. Then came the Seven Years' War, from 1756 to 1763, in which both St. Pierre and La Corne served admirably under the banner of the fleurs de lys. But all to no avail. The old French spirit had departed with the first and second generations of leaders and explorers, and there were none to take their places. Graft and greed had done their worst. The close of the war terminated the regime of the French in the Rainy River country for many years. Their place was taken at once by the conquerors, whose traders were advancing up Lake Superior even as the Frenchmen withdrew.

Water Lilies White and Gold

In 1823 Dr. John J. Bigsby was canoeing along the lake-and-river route between Lake Superior and Lake of the Woods, noting the beauties of the area as well as less interesting facts required by his official mission as assistant secretary of the British boundary commission. In practically every lake and pond he found water lilies and, like nearly all the other English travelers of his day, he admired and described them. "The water-lilies are superb," he wrote, "much the finest I have seen. They are about the size of a dahlia, for which they might be taken. They are double throughout, every row of petals diminishing by degrees, and passing gradually from the purest white to the highest lemon-colour. There is in the neighboring lakes a variety, wholly bright yellow."

By 1823 many men were on the flowing road of the fur traders. Bigsby was only one of scores of Englishmen to visit the north country in the years after 1763. English and Scotch merchants took over the fur trade with avidity even before the actual treaty of peace had been signed; and hardy explorers pushed on and on into the wilderness and out on the plains beyond the farthest discoveries of the French. By 1768 ground was being cleared at Grand Portage preparatory to erecting inland headquarters for the trade. Here, in succeeding years, a great fort of at least sixteen buildings, within frowning pickets, was constructed at the foot of high bluffs, between which Pigeon River plunged in rapids and waterfalls in its tempestuous course. These obstructions to navigation in the lower reaches of the stream made a long portage necessary, eight and more miles of sheer agony for voyageurs with their heavy burdens.

Up to Grand Portage from Montreal every July came hundreds of "pork eaters," novice or summertime voyageurs, in forty-foot canoes, stern flags flying and chansons floating on every breeze, as they brought the supplies needed for the North West Company's posts dotting the wilderness from Lake Superior north to the Arctic Sea and west to the mouths of the Fraser and Columbia rivers. From those posts on great and little lakes and streams came another group of voyageurs, lean, wiry "winterers," bringing in their smaller North canoes the result of the year's hunt, ninety-pound packs of beaver and other furs. The two groups, hundreds of hard-bitten men, had to be separated in their camping grounds outside the Grand Portage stockade; otherwise the ensuing quarrels and fights over their respective canoes, paddling abilities, and portaging prowess might have ended disastrously. But someone had only to begin singing a paddling song and unison was the enchanting result. These lighthearted, red-capped, French Canadian voyageurs in long, gay sashes and moccasins could never let many hours of a day pass without breaking into a folk tune — some haunting, jongleur composition, which had originated hundreds of years earlier in the Loire Valley and had been brought to New France in the seventeenth century. France seemed a long way off now to Canadian voyageurs, with Englishmen governing both their country and their trade, but they were as loyal to the new masters as they had been to the old; and so they went their accustomed way, chanting their usual songs and using the old French terms for everything pertaining to their business of voyaging.

Since all winterers had to pass up Rainy River in order to get to headquarters, many a fort was erected between Rat

Portage at the end of Lake of the Woods and the Lake Superior terminus. The first British traders arrived at the western end of Rainy Lake in the early 1760's and remained until 1763. In 1765 another trader tried to pass by the same route to the West, but the Rainy Lake Indians, now long destitute of white men's goods, stopped and plundered him and would not allow him to go on. He suffered the same fate the following year. Another attempt was made in the year 1767; some of the trade goods were left at Lac La Pluie to be traded with the natives, who permitted the Englishmen to proceed with the remainder; and the canoes penetrated beyond Lake Winnipeg. By 1787 two famous explorers, Alexander Henry the elder and Peter Pond, both colonial Americans, had passed Rainy Lake; and though in their reminiscences they made no mention of a post, one had surely been established, for in that year the greatest explorer of them all, Alexander Mackenzie, was there at the North West Company's fort. Thereafter that company had a Rainy River post until 1821, when it was absorbed by the Hudson's Bay Company. The latter began to lay plans for an establishment at Rainy Lake in 1777, but nothing was done until 1793. Then John McKay selected a spot near Manitou Rapids, a few miles below the falls, for the company's new establishment, and the fort was maintained until 1797.

Life in these trading posts can be glimpsed through old diaries, for practically every trading fort kept a journal. Many yellowing pages have survived to tell of the everyday life in stockaded posts, glowering at each other from various sites along the north bank of Rainy River, from its mouth to its beginning, as well as on Lake of the Woods and back in the forests. Many sites were occupied from time to time by the two organizations, especially on Rainy Lake and Lake of the Woods. McKay and his successors were the scribes for the Hudson's

Rainy River Country

Bay Company; their diaries and reports are preserved in London and date from 1793. Only one diary remains of all those penned by North West Company clerks and partners.

McKay tells how a site was selected, how the fort was constructed, how work was laid out day by day for the voyageurs, how Indians came and went, and how both master and men amused themselves in leisure hours. Nor is the weather forgotten, nor the larder's content — or lack of it.

McKay's post was some miles below the North West Company's establishment, which was about a mile and a half downriver from the lake and a little above the falls. Charles Boyer, in charge of the rival post, was on very friendly terms with McKay, and the men of the competing forts played football with one another, celebrated Christmas and New Year's together, and otherwise forgot trade rivalries occasionally. The Manitou Rapids post was built with the aid of a "long saw" for cutting the boards. It consisted of a "men's house," a "shop," a master's house without a doubt — though none is specifically mentioned in the diary — and a "stockade." An additional post was built by McKay the following year at the mouth of Rainy River and was named Ash House; and shortly Boyer likewise built a post there. The fiddler for the numerous dances held at these two new posts was, according to McKay, one of "the ordinariest negroes" he had ever seen, Robertson by name. As the well-known Bonga family of half Negro and half Indian blood originated in the Minnesota country with a slave whose master's name was Robertson, it is more than likely that the escaped slave found his way to this safe abode in the wilderness, where all things were free.

Frederick Shoults succeeded Boyer at the North West Company post at Rainy Lake; Peter Grant, a partner in the company, followed him. McKay having finally taken both himself and his house down-river to join his men at the mouth, no immediate competition was left at the outlet of the lake. By 1798 the Hudson's Bay Company had withdrawn its post completely; and the North West's post stood once more, solitary and imposing, "on the top of a steep bank of the river . . . two wooden Bastions in front flanking the Gate."

In 1797 and succeeding years during the next quarter century David Thompson was frequently at the Rainy Lake post on his trips to and from Grand Portage. This serious, able, religious astronomer and map maker, as an employee first of the Hudson's Bay Company and then, after 1797, of the North West Company, journeyed over a large part of northern North America taking observations for latitude and longitude and charting the area. The map on which he placed much of his data hung for years in the spacious dining hall at Fort William, where it spread before the eyes of the assembled three hundred diners the vast domain of "the Lords of the Lakes and the Forests," as the Nor'Westers were called. Not only Thompson's map, but also his detailed diaries of his explorations, have survived and reveal him, Minnesota's first map maker, a most painstaking and acute observer.

In 1800 Alexander Henry the younger, a nephew of the early explorer of the same name, passed Rainy Lake post, then under the command of Peter Grant, and wrote his impressions. Henry stopped at the fort for a day. "There is a good garden, well stocked with vegetables of various kinds — potatoes in particular, which are now eatable," he wrote. As usual, dancing occupied the evening hours: "The gentlemen danced until daybreak, all very merry."

By 1804 Hugh Faries was keeping the diary at the fort — a journal which most fortunately has survived. There was also a new rival fort, that of the X Y Company, an offshoot of the

North West Company during the last years of the eighteenth century and the first four years of the nineteenth. On January 12, 1805, Faries' diary records the arrival of a messenger bearing news of the merging of the two companies once more.

Faries directed not only the main post at the outlet of Rainy Lake, but also wintering houses and subsidiary establishments on neighboring lakes and streams, especially on Basswood Lake, Little Vermilion Lake, Lake of the Woods, and the Winnipeg River. Day after day he records how "old Amelle" was making "lisses," or white cedar frameworks for canoes; how "the men" were shaping snowshoes or dog sleds; how they made traps, or "drank all last night"; how "old Godin and Azure" went down-river to make wooden canoes; how the Athabasca River and the Swan River brigades and other flotillas of canoes from the far West and Northwest arrived and left; how outfits were made and sent to Eagle Lake, Clay Lake, Lake of the Woods, Mille Lacs, and other outlying posts; how runners came and went constantly between these establishments and the main fort, bearing news, letters, provisions, and so forth; how Indian and half-breed "girls" of voyageurs, clerks, and partners alike — including the *bourgeois*, or company partner, in charge of the district, as well as the diarist — rounded up Indians for the trade, made over a hundred pounds of maple sugar for the fort, netted snowshoes, and "were brought to bed of a fine" half-breed boy or girl; how Indians with such picturesque names as "The Liar," "Big Toad," "Frozen Foot," "Porcupine Tail," "Devil," "Big Rat," and "Young Toad" came and went, brought furs and meat, and took away "credits," or provisions and supplies for which their anticipated winter hunt was pledged; and how the master of this hive of industry watched over his hard-working but childlike *engagés*, gave them patent medicines like "Turling-

THE RAT PORTAGE, 1823
[From Bigsby's *The Shoe and Canoe.*]

SIR GEORGE SIMPSON ON A VOYAGE
[Courtesy Hudson's Bay Company.]

WIGWAM AND PAPOOSES, LAKE OF THE WOODS, 1901
[From a photograph owned by John Dobie.]

ton," or bled them when they were ill, punished and rewarded them, gave them minute instructions for every day's occupation, and directed their contest for furs with the neighboring X Y fort, superintended by one Lacombe.

Near by Little Vermilion Lake was a subpost evidently of great importance, for Peter Grant, the *bourgeois* or partner in charge of the whole district, spent the winter there, possibly near the ruins of Bourassa's stockaded post of 1736 and later. Another famous Nor'Wester and *bourgeois,* Dr. John McLoughlin, spent many winters there. In 1807 or thereabout he penned at this post a long account of "The Indians from Fort William to Lake of the Woods," which, unpublished, is still to be read in the library of McGill University in Montreal. Apparently at this same post on Vermilion Lake, on August 18, 1812, his son John was born. The junior McLoughlin, after medical training in France, was to have many bizarre experiences, terminating in his untimely assassination in Alaska some thirty years later—a tragedy that caused a permanent rift between Dr. McLoughlin and Sir George Simpson, governor in chief of the Hudson's Bay Company's territories. By the time of his son's murder, the doctor had long been the director of all Northwest coast matters for the company. Although his Oregon career is known by every school child, and his countenance, framed in its mass of white hair, appears on Oregon's centennial stamp, few know of his long and valuable service in the Minnesota country.

At this same time, across the Atlantic in that section of Scotland raided by John Paul Jones during the American Revolution, a young nobleman was growing increasingly interested in helping evicted tenants and other wretched people get a new start in life. Thomas, fifth earl of Selkirk, after several not-too-successful ventures, had finally decided to establish a colony in the center of North America, a region that he had come to know through the letters of a brother of one of his chief assistants, Miles Macdonell. John Macdonell had passed along the Rainy River canoe route as early as 1793, leaving a diary which tells of his experiences not only there, but later for many years on the Saskatchewan prairies of the Swan River district. While the fortunes of the Hudson's Bay Company were at low ebb during the European blockades of the Napoleonic era, Selkirk bought a controlling interest in the stock of the corporation; then he proceeded to engineer the cession to him of 116,000 square miles of the company's territories in North America. This cession, designated "Assiniboia" in 1811, included Rainy Lake, a large part of the basin of Rainy River, and the valley of the Red River of the North. Colonists arrived from Ireland, Scotland, the Hebrides, and the Orkneys in 1811 and settled in the lower Red River Valley. In later years others came from as far away as Switzerland. Those settlements were the beginnings of Winnipeg and St. Boniface.

There were many connections between the Rainy Lake post and the Red River settlements. Besides the canoe route joining the two areas by way of Lake of the Woods and the Winnipeg River, there was an overland trail, used time out of mind by Indians. It went up the Warroad River to a portage leading to Roseau River, and down that stream to the Red River. Fur traders had used it, mostly in winter, since La Vérendrye's time; now it became a well-used route for settlers and missionaries also.

The North West Company was not happy with Selkirk's decision. At first it attempted to block his purchase of stock through counterbuying by Sir Alexander Mackenzie, and later through still more obstructive tactics. When it became obvious that the settlement had been made and was going to continue, more forceful measures were taken, such as destroying the little Red River hamlets, killing their governor, Robert Semple, and taking prisoner many of the *bourgeois* and traders of the London company. The earl fought back, bringing up to Fort William disbanded troops from the Napoleonic battlefields, ramming open the fort's great gate with fixed bayonets, taking possession, and preparing to send troops and artillery to capture Rainy Lake post.

Peter Fidler was in charge of the attacking party at Rainy Lake late in 1816. The first attempt was unsuccessful, for when Fidler called upon the clerk in charge, J. W. Dease, to surrender, the latter refused. Fidler, lacking men to enforce his demand, returned to Fort William, secured more soldiers, two fieldpieces, and Captain D'Orsonnens, and returned to invest and blockade the fort. As Dease had only seven men with him, all depending on fishing and gathering wild rice for subsistence, he was forced to yield.

Now Lord Selkirk and his soldiers could advance from Fort William to attack the Nor'Westers in possession of the Red River settlements. He sent Miles Macdonell ahead with the soldiers to join D'Orsonnens' contingent, and the two men proceeded to the Red River by way of the Roseau River route, leaving Rainy Lake post on December 10 with twenty-eight men and two small fieldpieces. The military party soon routed the Nor'Westers; Lord Selkirk came up, via Rainy Lake post, the next spring; and by 1818 he was bringing in missionaries and French Canadian habitants to insure the permanence of his settlements. These men and women all reached Red River by the canoe route passing in front of Lac La Pluie post, which had been seized once more by the Nor'Westers after its short occupation by Lord Selkirk's men. Now, however, there was a Hudson's Bay post once more on Rainy River, which had been re-established in 1816, nearly twenty years after its abandonment. It was about this post, later called Fort Frances, that the city of the same name grew up.

The struggle between the rival fur companies continued until 1821, when a union was effected. Thereafter the combination was known as the Hudson's Bay Company, which, being the older and financially sounder of the two rivals, had really absorbed the North West Company. The North West fort above the falls was allowed to go to ruin, but its farm was retained and used by the fort at the cascade. One reason for the union was the appearance of a new and formidable rival, the American Fur Company, a New York corporation established in 1808, whose stock was all owned by John Jacob Astor. After the War of 1812 — the reverberations of which were heard clear to Rainy Lake through couriers sent thither by Tecumseh — this butcher's son from the Rhine country broke with his former partners of the North West Company and monopolized the fur trade south of the Great Lakes and Rainy River. His traders reached the northern Minnesota country at Sandy Lake, Red Lake, and elsewhere immediately after the war, but it was not until 1823 that his fort was built on the site of International Falls. He had posts also at Warroad, on Little Vermilion Lake, at Pembina, and at other places in the general neighborhood.

Missionaries also began to arrive. In 1816 the Reverend Pierre Antoine Tabeau reached Rainy Lake, despatched by the Catholic bishop of Quebec; but as he was an ardent partisan for the North West Company, Tabeau was not overzealous in carrying out the directions of his ordinary to press on and give spiritual succor to the residents of Red River. Therefore it was not until 1818 that the master of the Hudson's Bay Company post on Rainy River, Donald MacPherson, could write in his diary that missionaries had arrived from "below" and were going on to the new colony. These missionaries were the Reverend (soon Bishop) Joseph Norbert Provencher, Sèvére Dumoulin, and William Edge. Their letters to their bishop in Quebec mention the Rainy Lake posts, especially the new one, which Provencher describes as "still in its infancy." Dumoulin's work among Indians and half-breeds had a deep influence in the region, even as far as Rainy Lake, and he it was who laid the foundations for the later Catholic mission on Rainy River.

Succeeding Robert Logan, who penned the diary at the Hudson's Bay Company post for 1818–19, was Roderick McKenzie. His journal for 1819–20 devotes twenty-eight pages to the trip made by a whole body of French Canadian families migrating to Red River to settle, now that there were churches and priests there. This was the first mass migration to reach Lac La Pluie post, but many others were to follow, until railroads in the 1880's displaced birchbark canoes and other early forms of travel. As ever, the fort was the chief stopping place for weary, mosquito-bitten, sun-bronzed, half-starved travelers, who regarded it as an oasis in a great desert of trees and waters.

George Simpson and Nicholas Garry were two of the many important Hudson's Bay Company officials who passed down Rainy River at this time. Not yet overseas governor and not yet "Sir George," Simpson was already showing his flair for fast, spectacular travel, which would take him past Rainy Lake post nearly fifty times in the next forty years — years that would see the venerable company brought up to date under his revolutionary, businesslike ideas. Many a time his crack crew, flashing red blades, would push the brightly decorated bow of his big North canoe up to the pier of the post by the waterfall, to the ringing chorus of *En roulant ma boule* or the skirl of his Scotch bagpiper. Crossing a continent was like going to visit a friend, as far as Sir George was concerned, and he was almost as well acquainted with the gorges of the Columbia River as with the cherished flower gardens of his Isle Dorval in the St. Lawrence, near Montreal.

Garry was long deputy governor of the company in London, and for him Winnipeg was first called Fort Garry. In 1821 he made the difficult trip to Rainy Lake and beyond, keeping a most entertaining diary. He describes his stay at the Rainy River fort, his journey down the river, and his trip through Lake of the Woods, jotting down remarks about the voyageurs, their customs, and their songs, as well as keeping an eye out for the beauties of rock, flower, water, bird, and pine. Thus he writes: "Our Dinner Table was a hard Rock, no Table Cloth could be cleaner and the surrounding Plants and beautiful Flowers sweetening the Board. Before us the Waterfall, wild romantic, bold. . . . Foam loud Noise and chrystal Whiteness beautifully contrasted with the Black Pine. . . . The Wildness of the Scene was added to by the melancholy white headed Eagle hovering over our Board."

No diary for the Rainy Lake district has survived for the season 1822–23, but a long and valuable report was written by the master, Dr. John McLoughlin. He lists the Indians of his district — 107 men, 118 women, and 230 children, a total of 455, of whom 68 either lived south of the border or operated there as well as north of the line. His force consisted of twenty-four men, a guide, two interpreters, three clerks, and a chief trader, besides himself as chief factor. He reports in some detail the coming of the first American traders: George Johnston, of Sault Ste. Marie, at Vermilion Lake, and seven canoes, with ten men and five clerks, descending the Big Fork River to come and build directly opposite him on the river, in the very mist of the foaming cataract. One of the new clerks was the half-breed Pierre Coté; another was a Cadotte, probably Joseph. Both men became pioneer settlers of the Minnesota country. McLoughlin warned these American traders not to do business with Indians north of the river. In reply Coté wrote a letter accusing the Hudson's Bay Company men of trading south of the line, particularly at Roseau Lake.

The line was still in dispute, as a matter of fact. Indeed, this year of 1823 brought many distinguished scientists and government agents of Great Britain and the United States to Rainy Lake post, as they attempted to settle the forty-year-old controversy over the boundary provisions of the Treaty of Paris of 1783. Among the men were William Ferguson, George Washington Whistler, father of a great artist, and Major Joseph Delafield, all representing the United States; and David Thompson and Dr. John J. Bigsby, as well as others, representing Great Britain. At least two of these men have left accounts of their trips, which are more urbane and literary than the average trader's diary is; and, of course, Thompson's maps and diary entries are invaluable.

The most extraordinary part of the whole boundary controversy, from Maine to Minnesota, was that section of the treaty of 1783 which provided that the dividing line should follow the "usual water communication" to the northwestern-most angle of Lake of the Woods and thence due west until it intercepted the Mississippi! The occasion for this pursuit of an elusive river was the map used by the treaty commissioners. Published in 1755 by John Mitchell, it showed the Mississippi apparently rising in Canada, under an insert map that covered the northwest portion of the Minnesota country.

Rainy River Country

Since the rest of the Mississippi ran generally from north to south, the commissioners obviously concluded that the portion under the insert map did likewise. Actually, of course, the river rises much farther south and flows northward until it bends back toward the south.

Various attempts to make an adjustment were unsuccessful before the close of the War of 1812. After that conflict ended, the Convention of 1818 between Great Britain and the United States determined the boundary line west of Lake of the Woods. It was to be the forty-ninth parallel from the point where a line, dropped due south from the northwesternmost angle of the Lake of the Woods, should intercept that parallel. The chase after the Mississippi was ended, but the northwesternmost angle of the Lake of the Woods, a lake of thousands of islands and many bays, remained to be agreed upon.

From 1817 to 1823, or a little later, boundary surveyors and agents of both countries traveled from Nova Scotia to Lake of the Woods, mapping the region of the boundary line in great detail. By 1822 they were in Lake Superior trying to find "Long Lake," which, by the provisions of the treaty, was the Lake Superior terminus of the "usual water communication" between that body of water and Lake of the Woods. In 1823 they spent the entire season on the canoe routes leading to Lake of the Woods. By that time their pretensions were greater than in earlier years. Indeed, Major Delafield's recently published diaries and papers reveal that he decided to outdo the English when he found that they, following David Thompson, claimed that the usual canoe route of 1783 followed up the St. Louis River from Fond du Lac, where Duluth is now. Delafield countered with the claim that the old canoe route of the treaty was the Kaministiquia River. Thus the entire Arrowhead area of today was in dispute. Actually, Delafield

LAKE SHEBANDOWAN, DAWSON ROUTE

[From Gibbons' *Steel of Empire* (copyright 1935). By special permission of the Bobbs-Merrill Company.]

TYPICAL CANOE ROUTE SCENE, 1823

[From Bigsby's *The Shoe and Canoe*.]

FORT FRANCES, 1857

[From Hind's *Red River Expedition*.]

HUDSON'S BAY COMPANY POST AT RAT PORTAGE, 1857

[From Hind's *Red River Expedition*.]

BIRCH BARK CANOES UNDER CONSTRUCTION

[From a photograph owned by John Dobie.]

was on much more solid ground than were his opponents, for the old French route *was* up the Kaministiquia River to Lac La Croix, where it joined the Grand Portage route. Moreover, since 1802 or thereabout, Grand Portage had been abandoned by British traders in favor of Fort William at the mouth of the Kaministiquia, since that river was entirely within British territory. All canoe traffic at the Grand Portage had to proceed for eight or nine miles over American soil and might be subjected to customs duties.

Although there was much fraternization among the numerous representatives of the two countries that summer of 1823, as they canoed up and down the lakes and streams between Fort William, Fond du Lac, and Rat Portage, no agreement was reached as to "the usual water communication" of the treaty of 1783, except in the stretch of the boundary between Rainy Lake and Lake of the Woods. There everyone agreed that Rainy River was the boundary. For the rest, it took nearly twenty more years for a definite line to be traced. In 1842 Daniel Webster and Lord Ashburton made a treaty which settled the boundary dispute and recognized the old Pigeon River canoe route to Rainy Lake as the "usual water communication." It also stipulated that the old portages, scenes of so much friendly rivalry in voyaging days, were to be common highways for the nationals of both countries. So they remain to this day.

Another boundary matter was being settled in that year, 1823. Since the Convention of 1818 stipulated that the forty-ninth parallel was to serve for the boundary line west of Lake of the Woods, the United States government sent a military party under Major Stephen H. Long to determine exactly where that line lay. Having passed down the Red River Valley to the Selkirk settlements, Long decided to return via the canoe route. Thus his party added to the relative congestion of traffic on Rainy River that summer; and he, too, published an account of his journey written by the secretary of the expedition, William H. Keating.

As if that summer's activities did not have enough scribes, an account of John Tanner's near murder that season just east of Rainy Lake, and the enthralling story of his life in the region between Lake Superior and the Missouri from 1790 to 1823 were soon dictated by him to an army surgeon and published. When Tanner, a blue-eyed lad of about ten years, was stolen from his father's frontier home in Kentucky about 1789, everyone in the civilized world who knew about the event concluded that he had been killed. Instead, he was abducted, because an Indian mother had just lost her boy and could not rest till she had another son in his place. John was taken successively to Detroit, Mackinac, and Grand Portage, and, finally, to the Rainy River region. There he grew up as an Indian, married two Indian women, had Indian children, and was a native in most respects. In 1823, however, urged on by white men, he was leaving for his native land, when he was ambushed, shot, and nearly killed. Found by a trader along the canoe track, he was taken back to Lac La Pluie fort to be treated medically by Dr. McLoughlin. There all the travelers of that busy season met him, and in their accounts they tell his story. His own dictated reminiscences put a reader under the spell of seeing through an Indian's eyes the lakes, rocks, fish and other wild life, the Indians and the white traders of the Rainy River country between 1790 and 1823. Tanner spent the remainder of his life at Sault Ste. Marie as an interpreter.

Tanner's farm, so to speak, had been an island in Lake of the Woods, then called Plantation Island, probably Garden Island today. For generations Indians had cultivated their corn and other crops there. In 1826 the man in charge of the Rainy

Lake post, John Dugald Cameron, devoted to that island and some other topics thirty-two pages of his report to London headquarters. Let no one believe that fur traders were illiterate men. Cameron was the son of a Scotch loyalist of Schenectady, New York, who fled to Canada at the time of the American Revolution. There John was born in 1777. After years of service with the North West Company in the Nipigon, Lake Winnipeg, and Ile-a-la Crosse departments, he was made a chief factor at the time of union of the two companies in 1821 and was in charge of the Columbia district until 1824. Then he and Dr. McLoughlin exchanged posts. From 1824 until 1832 Cameron was in charge of the Lac La Pluie district. When he retired to Grafton, Ontario, in 1846, he took his Indian wife and family with him. Sir George Simpson, who was not given to excessive praise of the men in his jurisdiction — for all of whom, it may be added, he kept a "character book" — writes thus of Cameron: "Strictly correct in all his conduct and dealings, and possesses much influence over the Natives; Speaks Salteaux [*Chippewa*] well, and is one of our best Indian Traders, but in other respects not a man of business; nor well educated, yet possesses a good deal of general information having read almost every Book that ever came within his reach."

It is Cameron, in his report of 1825–26, who tells us of the region's flora and fauna, including its fishes. He is especially detailed in the matter of beaver, which was almost extinct, according to his report, because of the fearful forest fires of 1803–04, the preying of wolverines, and "their own plagues." Cameron's post boasted a cow, an ox, a bull calf, four horses, five sows, and two boars. Under his direction there were four other men in the district above the rank of voyageur, and about twenty voyageurs.

Other interesting characters in this period of Rainy Lake

history were Simon McGillivray, William Morrison, and the Roy family. Young McGillivray, half-breed son of one of the barons of the trade, William McGillivray, for whom Fort William is named, was the author of the 1825 report for the Lac La Pluie district. Educated, with European travel in his background, the young fellow was noted by Major Delafield in 1823 as incongruous in such a setting, being "the most accomplished & intelligent of any [half-breed] I have met." His wife was a daughter of Vincent Roy and a sister of Vincent Roy, Jr., both of whom feature largely in the valley's history for many years.

Practically all the travelers in the nineteenth century mention the Roy farm at the mouth of the Little Fork River, on its eastern bank. It was one of the few cleared spots on the southern bank of Rainy River as late as 1890. Delafield in 1823 described the place and its owner: "Mr. Roy, a Frenchman who has settled here, an old North West servant who married a native & preferred to reside in the interior when free. He has a large family. His daughter is the wife of Mr. McGillivray at the fort. . . . There is some ground cleared around his log hut & I presume with the good fishery that is before his door he is enabled to live by his labor." Dr. Bigsby in the same year mentions Roy and his farm: "an extensive meadow is all the farm I saw, but I did not land." Probably there were horses on this farm; at least, late in 1817, MacPherson tells in his diary at the Hudson's Bay Company post how Roy had just appeared with thirteen horses, which he had driven or led up from Fond du Lac to sell to the Nor'Westers.

William Morrison is better known than McGillivray and the Roys, for he and his brother Allan later settled in Minnesota, which named one of its counties in their honor. McGillivray records on October 1, 1825, that William Morrison and eleven men had arrived on the site of International Falls. "His presence gave us to presume this would be a stirring campaign," McGillivray wrote, for he knew that he was facing a veteran Nor'Wester, who somehow had been overlooked in the settlement between the two British companies at the time of their union in 1821. John Jacob Astor had been astute enough to employ Morrison, and now the canny old trader was back in his former hunting grounds, but working for the opposition. It was Morrison who claimed to be the first white man to reach Lake Itasca and recognize it as the source of the Mississippi River. This was in 1804, more than a quarter century before Henry R. Schoolcraft looked upon the lake; but Schoolcraft made his discovery known at once, whereas Morrison made no claim prior to Schoolcraft's arrival. Therefore to Schoolcraft goes the honor of discovering the true head of the Mississippi in 1832.

Other significant traders in the area were employees of John Jacob Astor: the Davenports, the Beaulieus, the Roussains, the Johnstons of Sault Ste. Marie, and others. Much can be learned of them and their posts on Red Lake, Lake of the Woods, Rainy River, and the Vermilion lakes by browsing through the diaries and reports kept at the Hudson's Bay Company fort at the outlet of Rainy Lake, still called Lac La Pluie post in 1830. In that year George Simpson stopped at the fort, and with him was his bride, Frances. Cameron records the visit of this "lovely and accomplished Lady," and a little later, on September 25, reports: "This Morning at Sun rise the New flag Staff was up and the New Flag hoisted. In the mean time a flaccon of Spirits was broken and Spilled on the foot of the Staff, and the Fort named Fort Frances in honour of Mrs. Simpsons Christian Name. All the Whites gave three Hearty Cheers — and the Indians fired above 300 Shots."

Rainy River Country

Another person, who would create a name and fame for himself as time went on, arrived that year, 1830, on the site of International Falls. This was Dr. Charles William Wulff Borup, who had been educated in Copenhagen and was now out in the wilderness as a fur trader. Cameron was more than ordinarily interested in the newcomer and in his diary speculates much concerning him. At first he must be a "Constable sent in to seize Mainville for the *Drubbing* he gave a Yankee interpreter last spring." Mainville, one of Cameron's men, must have had a very guilty conscience! Later Cameron had a visit from the physician and learned that Borup was then in charge of the rival post; "the principle post in charge of a Novice (for such we must suppose Doctor Wulff to be)!" he exclaimed.

By New Year's Day, 1831, Cameron was truly disturbed by the Dane's activities, for the doctor was upsetting a long-established custom. The French had been given to celebrating that day in true Gallic fashion, even to kissing all the Indian women and bestowing drinks and gifts on their husbands. Now the European doctor, accustomed to think of women, no less than their husbands, as human beings, gave presents to the squaws as well as the braves. This caused Cameron, the perturbed scion of a Scotch family, to write: "I believe he has a good deal of the Simpleton in his Economy," giving presents to all the women, which "was altogether a new thing to Indian Women, and as a matter of course, the Doctor now passes for a great and Charitable Chief."

In 1833 an agreement was reached between the American Fur Company and the Hudson's Bay Company, whereby for a good sum of money the Yankees agreed to withdraw their competition along Minnesota's present boundary. Thereafter Dr. Borup became a resident of La Pointe on Madeline Island on the south shore of Lake Superior, until he migrated to St.

Paul and became a much esteemed banker there in the 1850's.

For about a decade after 1833 there were few, if any, American traders along border waters. Travelers were still numerous, however. On June 12, 1837, the post diarist records that young "Dr. McLoughlin, son of Chief Factor McLoughlin embarked in . . . Boats on his way down to Fort Alexander" at the mouth of Winnipeg River. In 1836 this young man had been part of a strange filibustering expedition, which a man calling himself "General" James Dickson had led across the northern Minnesota country. The "general" was recruiting men for his "army," with which he proposed to capture Mexican territory about Santa Fe. In Montreal he had secured as "officers" many disaffected sons of fur traders — half-breeds for the most part. Young McLoughlin, back prematurely from an unfinished medical course in Paris, was one of them. At the Red River settlements, where Dickson aimed to secure the privates of his "army" among the numerous half-breeds there, the expedition broke up, for Hudson's Bay Company officials along the line of march had sent fast couriers to Red River, warning of what was afoot. As a means of disrupting the scheme, the company offered jobs to many of the "officers," including McLoughlin. He accepted a position in the far Northwest and was now, in June, 1837, on his way to his new job, saying farewell forever, as it turned out, to this place of his birth.

As McLoughlin's boats went downstream from the fort, their occupants must have noticed what William Sinclair, the clerk at the fort, noted in his diary that month, namely, that "the little Settlement of the *little* Forks below this is almost wholy abandoned by its inhabitants — one Simon Sayer only remaining to take care of the remaining property . . . during the proprietor's absence (Vincent Roy)." Young Roy had gone temporarily to the Sault. "Old Vincent Roy is also off for Red River where he intends to settle and end his well spent life," wrote Sinclair.

For almost a century fur traders had dominated the scene in the Rainy River country. Now missionaries returned to resume the work begun by the three Jesuits at Fort St. Charles a century before. The Red River pastors, Provencher and Dumoulin, had passed through occasionally. Dumoulin, dejected and unhappy, had passed for the last time in 1823. After he had spent five successful years at Pembina on the Red River, Long's expedition had settled the question of the nationality of the little settlement of Indians and half-breeds where his Pembina chapel stood. As the United States could claim jurisdiction, the Canadian mission was withdrawn. Thereupon, the young missionary asked to be recalled. His place was not filled until 1831, when Georges Antoine Belcourt arrived and made himself a power from Rainy Lake to the plains far beyond the Red River settlements. On May 31, 1838, for example, the fort diarist records: "On the 25th Inst. Chief Factor McDonell and the Revd G. A. Bellcourt both from Fort Alexander" arrived, "the latter . . . on a Missionary visit to the Indians & people of this post and proposes to remain a month amongst us."

About the same period two other Catholic missionaries spent a little time at the fort, both on their way to the Oregon country; for Rainy Lake was by that time a way station for practically everyone en route to that fabulous land where Dr. McLoughlin reigned supreme. The Oregon Trail was hardly established as yet and would not supplant this old route for several years. The wayfarers of May and June, 1838, were the Reverend Francis Norbert Blanchet and the Reverend Modest Demers. During the latter's stay at Fort Frances seven children

34

THE RED RIVER EXPEDITION ON A PORTAGE

[From a photograph of a painting by Frances Hopkins in the Public Archives of Canada.]

THE ISLINGTON MISSION NEAR RAT PORTAGE

[From Hind's *Red River Expedition*.]

were baptized. In later years both men became bishops in their new charges beyond the Rocky Mountains.

But Catholic missionaries no longer had the Rainy Lake field all to themselves. Already a scholarly, far-visioned Wesleyan missionary, the Reverend James Evans, had been at the post and had concluded that the field was ripe for harvesting. Therefore, in 1839 he returned, accompanied by Pate-tah-se-gay, better known as Peter Jacobs; and with him, too, were Thomas Hurlburt and Henry Steinham, the latter "a member of the same tribe" as Jacobs, according to the annual report of the Wesleyan Missionary Society of London, and, like him, "a young man of much promise," who "acts as Schoolmaster and Interpreter." From 1839 to 1843 William Mason was in charge of this mission; then Jacobs became the leading missionary until he went to Lac Seul in the hinterland, when the Rainy River mission was abandoned in 1846. Evans died after a brilliant career farther in the interior, particularly at Norway House, the headquarters of the mission. There, close to the Hudson's Bay Company fort, he built a village of converts, reduced the Cree language to an alphabet, and even established a press and printed religious data in the native tongue. He was the first missionary to follow the fur traders into the heart of the beaver country, the far-famed Athabasca country. Probably his knowledge of that distant land under the Arctic Circle stemmed from his first visits to Fort Frances, since it was there that the Athabasca House had been a feature from the beginning of English trade. The voyageurs from Lake Athabasca could not get to Grand Portage and Fort William in one season and return; therefore a depot for them had been a separate unit of the Rainy Lake posts for generations. Perhaps these much-traveled, Gasconading voyageurs, who were admittedly the best in the fur trade, had aroused Evans' interest by their

ᐁᐯ ᐃᐯ ᐃᑕ ᐃᐱ ᐃ ᐲ ᐊ ᐊᐅᑲ

ᐯᐁ ᐯ ᐁᐅ ᐱ ᐱᐸ ᑲ

ᑭᓇ ᐁ
1841

tall tales, red plumes, and strutting manners at Athabasca House.

It was not the post nor the voyageurs that lured the missionaries, especially the Wesleyans, to Rainy Lake; rather it was the fact that this was the religious gathering place for hundreds of Indians, both Cree and Chippewa. One of the reports of this mission, published at headquarters in London for the year 1841, explains the station's importance: *"Rainy Lake,* or Lac la Pluie, is one of the most important establishments on the East of the Rocky Mountains. There are generally from two to five hundred Indians in the immediate vicinity of the company's Fort; and during a part of the year their numbers may be estimated at not less than two thousand. Rainy Lake is one of the principal places in the country for holding the Great Indian Medicine Feasts. . . . The *Mittay* or *Medicine-men* are strongly opposed" to the Christian religion. So strong, indeed, was the Indians' faith in their own religion, that little success was achieved by any of the missionaries, and the stations were abandoned by 1847, both by Catholics and Protestants. The Wesleyan mission, however, was re-established in 1853 under Allen Salt, and it persisted until 1858.

A little more success was had at Wabassimong, or White Dog, some miles downstream from Rat Portage on a small trough of agricultural land in the otherwise rocky gorges and inhospitable ledges of Winnipeg River. Although Belcourt's mission there in the 1830's and early 1840's was not rewarding and was given up, Islington Mission of the Established Church took over the site in 1855 and made it prosper.

At some time in the period after the War of 1812 a fur-trading post had been established at Rat Portage. Although early clerks at Rainy Lake post mention the Rat portage in their diaries and reports, no reference to a fort is to be found for many years. Simon McGillivray, writing about the boundary dispute in 1825, explains the origin of the odd name: "Our most valuable hunting grounds including the Rat Country in the Lake of the Woods" would be lost, if the United States pressed its claims to a successful conclusion. In other words, Rat Portage was the carrying place to the muskrat country. Like Fort Frances, Rat Portage post grew slowly into a hamlet, and finally into a town; but, unlike Fort Frances, the original name did not last. Today Rat Portage is Kenora, a fabricated name, composed of the first two letters of three neighboring place names: Keewatin, Norman, and Rat Portage.

In 1847 an English traveler, Frederick Ulric Graham, found Rat Portage to consist of "a house and two stores, a miserable looking place," presided over by Donald McKenzie, otherwise "the Major." This sobriquet was the result of McKenzie's soldiering experiences as a lieutenant in the Peninsula Campaign of the Napoleonic wars, of which he loved to talk, especially of the battle of Corunna, where Sir John Moore was killed. According to Graham, McKenzie had "afterwards joined the Hudson's Bay Company, had married a half-breed, and had been thirty years in the service. He appeared very proud of his dogs and cattle, talked a great deal about Corunna, and gave us a capital breakfast, in which cream and white fish predominated, or rather formed the whole." McKenzie was in charge of Rat Portage from 1845 to 1850, and was in the company's service as early as 1818.

Of course, this was not the only post, nor the first, on Lake of the Woods. Substations of both companies' establishments on Rainy River were maintained until the union in 1821; thereafter the Hudson's Bay Company competed with the American Fur Company until 1833. Numerous posts are mentioned in diaries and reports of fur traders and travelers. Whitefish Lake, or Bay, nearly always supported a post; Lac Plat, or Shoal Lake, was another favorite place; so was War- road, on the site of the present place of that name. The Thomas McMurray, later the son-in-law of James Evans, was the trader at Whitefish Bay for the season 1824–25; the diaries kept at Rainy Lake post mention several other post masters.

McLoughlin in 1823 explained that in "Lake of the Woods we used to keep one Post, one year on the South Side and the next on the North, but as the South side belongs to the Ameri- cans, we cannot go to our former place, War road." He also stated that "White Fish Lake — the other Post in this district, is situated on the North Shore of Lake of the Woods, and is so called from their [*sic*] being a good White Fish Fishery in years of low water and is about sixty miles from the entrance of Rainy Lake" by the "back road," or canoe route up North- west Bay of Rainy Lake and thence by water and portage. "I got in 1814–5 about four hundred Bushels of [wild] Rice from this place," he added reminiscently.

McMurray spent the seasons from 1825 to 1831 at another post on the same lake, not specifically located but carefully distinguished in the diaries and reports from the posts on Whitefish Bay and Shoal Lake. Perhaps this was Rat Portage. From McLoughlin's remarks one can infer that after 1823 there were only American traders on the south shore of the lake. In 1825 Morrison decided to establish an American Fur Company post at Warroad, with one clerk and two men. But this spot must also have been abandoned by 1833, when all American opposition on the border was bought off by the Hudson's Bay Company.

By the time the agreement between Ramsay Crooks, presi- dent of the American Fur Company, and the Hudson's Bay

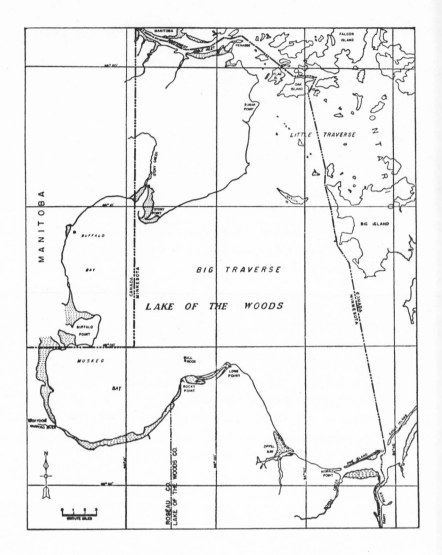

INTERNATIONAL BOUNDARY AT LAKE OF THE WOODS

Company had terminated in the 1840's, it had been decided by the Webster-Ashburton Treaty of 1842 that the "northwesternmost angle" of Lake of the Woods was a certain spot on a piece of land now called the Northwest Angle, a part of Minnesota jutting into the lake far to the north of the other forty-seven states, and completely separated from them by water and Canada. Thus the site of old Fort St. Charles became American.

The Northwest Angle, covering about 130 square miles of territory, has been famous in American history for Fort St. Charles and for a boundary dispute; in Canadian history it was also important, as the water terminus of the so-called Dawson Route from Lake Superior to Winnipeg, and it was the site of a noted Indian treaty in 1873. Moreover, it carried a Hudson's Bay trading post probably longer than any other bit of American territory. Men like George McPherson, Peter Sinclair, Louis Kittson, and John E. Sinclair, who were in charge at Rat Portage after 1858, often served also at Northwest Angle post. After the season of 1877–78 it no longer appears on the list of company establishments; but as recently as October, 1885, Herbert Williams left Rat Portage with three bargeloads of winter supplies for a Northwest Angle post.

Eternal Pines

WITH THE mid-century the fur trade began to wane. Steamboats, canals, railroads, spelled doom to voyageurs and birchbark canoes. They also meant a rapidly dwindling wilderness, for the frontier of settlement in both the United States and Canada moved now at an accelerated pace. Gold was discovered, not only in California, but also on the Canadian west coast. Men's thoughts turned to surer ways than canoe routes to link East and West, and to the possibility of precious metals in many parts of the continent.

In the late 1840's a geological survey was made in northern Minnesota by the United States government. David Dale Owen's surveyors spied out the borderland, despite myriads of green caterpillars that fell down their necks, dropped into their food, and left the beautiful countryside as brown and desolate in midsummer as though fires had passed over the land. But they found iron ore and indications of other metals. Other travelers of the same period noted the desolation and its unlovely cause, but failed to note the minerals. Among the wayfarers were two young gentlemen, soon to be titled, from another border, the Scottish March — Frederick Graham and Vincent Rowland Corbet — bound for big-game hunting around Fort Edmonton. Graham, from Netherby Hall, has left behind a narrative of the two men's experiences, which is one of the most informal, chatty, and modern diaries of all the many accounts of the border country that have survived. Leaving Fort Frances, where he had been entertained by James Isbister in lieu of the absent chief factor, Nicol Finlayson, Graham and his party "ran down the Lac de Pluie river, a fine broad stream, with rich land on either shore." He was seeing the region through Scottish eyes: "It is the 'march' between British and American lands, and the forest on both banks consists of birch and hard wood instead of the eternal pine forests, which we have hitherto passed through." At Manitou Rapids he found the "Indians . . . fishing in the rapid, through which we shot, and passed too quickly for any of them to come off to us. The site of the Indian camp last passed was famous among the tribe as being sacred to the 'Manitou,' or god, covered with tombs, or cairns, apparently raised in the same manner as those in the Highlands, and, like them, said to be the graves of the great warriors of former days."

Another traveler passed about the same time — Paul Kane, the Canadian artist, whose sketches and canvases are highly prized today. He, too, was bound for Fort Edmonton and the far West, and, like Graham, he traveled in the company of Sir George Simpson, who was on another of his whirlwind tours of the company's posts. Kane not only kept a diary and painted and sketched constantly, but he published a book on his trip in the years from 1845 to 1848, which told of his stay at Fort Frances. The fort, he writes, has "usually about 250 Indians in its neighbourhood, who have a half-breed missionary of the Methodist church resident amongst them." The Indians lived there "as at Rat Portage, on rice, fish, and rabbits."

In 1848 Sir John Richardson was on Rainy River — for the third time — en route, as usual, to the Arctic. On this journey autumn glories inspired him to write that "the various maples, oaks, sumachs, ampelopsis, cornel bushes, and other trees and shrubs whose leaves before they fall assume glowing tints of orange and red, render the woodland views equal, if not superior, to the finest that I have seen elsewhere on the

American continent, from Florida northwards." He was an accomplished botanist, as well as a famous ornithologist. Therefore he noted "showy asters," sunflowers, hyssops, gentians, mints, and other "gay flowers" adorning Rainy River's banks. Mentioned in his four-volume work on the fauna of northern North America are some specimens found in the vicinity of Rainy Lake. "We gathered *Opuntia glomera* [*prickly pear cactus*], or *crapaud verd* [*green toad*] of the voyageurs, on the Lake of the Woods," he wrote. Richardson had already watched the spring come, as he traveled from Lake Superior to Lake of the Woods that year, and he wrote most appreciatively of its soft, lacelike forms and delicate shades. Had he passed in later spring or early summer, he would doubtless have written ecstatically of the arbutus, pink lady's-slippers and other exotic orchids, lupines, bright wood lilies, and wild roses.

Another sensitive soul saw the region in 1859, the young Chicago naturalist, Robert Kennicott, whose brief but startlingly brilliant career was cut short in 1866, after several years in the Arctic. No one has ever penned so gay an account of voyageurs and voyaging as he. Just before reaching Rainy Lake, his companion, one Hubbard, "found the nest of a ruffed grouse, containing five eggs. These our cook used in making our *galette*, thereby giving us quite a treat. This galette is the only form of bread used on a voyage, that is, when voyageurs are so fortunate as to have any flour at all." Then he describes how it is made in that area: "the flour bag is opened, and a small hollow made in the flour, into which a little water is poured, and the dough is thus mixed in the bag; nothing is added, except perhaps some dirt from the cook's *unwashed* hands with which he kneads it into flat cakes, which are baked before the fire in a frying pan, or cooked in grease. . . . There is no denying that voyageurs are not apt to be very cleanly . . . but it is wonderful how any fastidiousness . . . wears off when a traveler is voyaging in the wilderness."

The guide, "old Baptiste," was a great favorite of his. "During our first day among the rapids old Baptiste, the guide, was constantly in great glee, and always laughed when entering a bad rapid." Evidently the voyageurs liked Kennicott, too, for on Lac La Croix they paid him the compliment of erecting a "lob stick, or may pole," in honor of him and Hubbard. "A tall pine, standing out on a point in the lake, was climbed by one of the voyageurs, who, with an ax, cut off all the branches, excepting a tuft at the top, thus rendering it very conspicuous. As we paddled off it was saluted with three cheers and the discharge of the guns, we, of course, being expected to acknowledge the compliment by a treat at the first opportunity." Those who have wondered why Lobstick Island in Rainy Lake, near Haymarsh Bay, is so called will now comprehend the origin of the unusual term.

Kennicott's is the first migration and nesting list of birds for Minnesota's border country, and so his diary has great value for scientists. He also lists the trees, shrubs, flowering plants, mosses, lichens, insects, rodents, and so forth — all with their Latin names, as a rule, so that there is no chance for misconception. The remarkable thing is that so young a man — he was twenty-four when he made the journey — could have had so extensive a knowledge in so many fields of natural history. But he had made his mark in the scientific world when he was only eighteen, and he was already famous in natural-history circles throughout the country when he journeyed with such delight and appreciation "down North" in 1859.

Rainy River Country

A new era began on the border in 1870. It might be called the "Steamboat Era." For, with the opening of the Dawson Route, steamboats began to take the place of canoes and York boats. The route takes its name from Simon J. Dawson, who as surveyor, with Henry Y. Hind as geologist and naturalist, was sent by the Canadian government in 1857 to explore the region between Lake Superior and the Red River settlements. The government's hope was that an all-Canada route of travel might be found to expedite migration to western British America, especially British Columbia, and hold it for the empire against the obviously increasing aggressiveness of American frontiersmen in Minnesota and elsewhere. Minnesota had become a territory in 1849, stretching to the Missouri, and in 1858 she entered the union with her western boundary at the Red River. Already a certain element in her population was looking for more worlds to conquer. This spirit of unrest perturbed Ottawa and London, and so two other expeditions were sent out the same year that Hind and Dawson made their trip, one by the Canadian government to the plains, and the other, under Captain John Palliser, by the British government. The result was a recommendation that the old canoe route between Lake Superior and Lake of the Woods be improved and that a road be laid out between the Northwest Angle and Winnipeg.

In the next decade some progress was made in this transportation program, but it was an event of 1870 that really established the Dawson Trail. Until 1869 much of northwestern North America had been within the territories of the Hudson's Bay Company; then they were transferred, with a few exceptions, to the Dominion. As the residents were not consulted in this transfer of lands, and because they were disgruntled on other points, they were shortly in armed rebellion under a half-breed leader, Louis Riel. To quell the uprising, an expeditionary force of about 1400 men was sent to Manitoba from Toronto, under the command of Lieutenant Colonel (later Lord) Garnet Wolseley. Passing by rail to Lake Huron and thence by vessel they arrived at Prince Arthur's Landing, now Port Arthur. There the new Dawson Trail began.

The story of the expedition thereafter is an extraordinary one. An Irishman, Peter O'Leary, traveling the route in 1874. pays tribute to the organizing mind of the leader who, with greenhorns on waters ordinarily navigated by skilled voyageurs, took his troops unscathed along border waters, building roads, portages, and blockhouses as he went. O'Leary marveled as he journeyed: "everywhere along the route [are] traces of Sir Garnet Wolseley's expedition. . . . block houses in ruins that were built by the expedition as commassariat stores, trees laying rotted that were cut down to make the road — it was surveyed by Mr. Dawson . . . but for building bridges, clearing the bush, removing boulders and rocks, in fact building the road, the honour is alone due to Sir Garnet, and those who served under him, assisted by Mr. Dawson . . . a gigantic undertaking . . . of those warrior road-makers."

Yet the expedition made great speed, despite all its building activities, for it left Thunder Bay on Lake Superior on July 1 and reached Fort Garry on August 24. The halt at Fort Frances was a notable one. Captain G. L. Huyshe wrote: "Glad indeed were we to see signs of the abode of man after the desolate and inhospitable region we had passed through. . . . this green and fertile oasis in the midst of the desert of rock, forest, and water, was like a glimpse of the Promised Land." For five days the officers "revelled in green peas, young potatoes, and cabbages, most agreeable antidotes to the scorbutic tendencies of salt pork."

Before Colonel Wolseley left Fort Frances, he saw all the

regular troops and the first two brigades of militia pass on. Every departing brigade left its surplus stores to form a depot of supplies at Fort Frances. Moreover, a hospital was established, capable of accommodating thirty-six patients, and a field oven was put up and a bakery started, by means of which the rear brigades were served with fresh bread, a pleasant change after weeks on hard biscuit. A company of the First Ontario Rifles, left as a garrison, pitched its camp on the grassy bank of the river close by the fort.

The value of the route was evident to all, and the Dominion proceeded at once to make it the link between East and West. Roads were made; portages were improved and supplied with carts and vans, and sometimes even with hostelries; and, most important, steam tugs were placed on many of the lakes. It was thus that steam navigation began on Rainy Lake, Rainy River, and Lake of the Woods, not to mention the lakes to the east.

Immigrants to the opening West poured over the Dawson Trail. O'Leary tells of them in his book, published in 1875; and an even earlier account had appeared, written by the Reverend George M. Grant and published in 1873. When British Columbia agreed to enter the Dominion in July, 1871, one condition of union was the construction of a transcontinental railroad. Sandford Fleming was put in charge of the construction of the proposed line, and he made a tour of inspection in 1872, accompanied by Grant. The two books give in detail the story of how the authors journeyed on the old canoe route from Fort William to Lake of the Woods — now towed by the new tugs, now proceeding as of old in canoes or boats, especially while *saulting* rapids. On Lake Windegoostigwan there was a "station" and a "station-keeper," with a tent set up for emigrants. On the next portage but one there was a wagon on a new portage road, with a man from Glengarry in charge. He declared that he had liked the winter he had just spent there. There was a steam launch on Mille Lacs, and there were tugs on many lakes, including Shebandowan, Kashabowie, Lac La Croix, Namakan, Rainy Lake, Rainy River, and Lake of the Woods. The steamer on Rainy Lake was probably the "Louise Thompson"; the one on Lake of the Woods may well have been the "Lady of the Lake."

The imagination is staggered at the thought of how the material and machinery for these vessels were carried to those almost inaccessible lakes, probably in the dead of winter over snow and ice. One is equally amazed at the cheerful acceptance of the route by so many persons accustomed to life in England, Ireland, Europe, and Canada. Grant tells of one old emigrant lady in his party who was eighty-five years old. There were also two young men traveling for pleasure; but most of the travelers were going to a new life on the prairies.

The journey from Prince Arthur's Landing to Fort Frances, the first stop, took about six days. The next overnight stop was the Hudson's Bay Company post on lower Rainy River, dubbed "Hungry Hall" at this time. It seems to have been near the site of Ash House, McKay's post in the 1790's. A night was spent on an island in Lake of the Woods, and the final day of the water route took the travelers to terra firma once more, just where La Vérendrye and his company had built their abode, old Fort St. Charles. There a new road had been constructed to Winnipeg, and there were teams to haul passengers and their luggage.

A distinguished party went over this end of the route in 1877, Lord Dufferin, the governor general of Canada, and his wife and party. Lady Dufferin later published an account of her trip. The corduroy road was in sad need of repair by that time, and Lady Dufferin describes it well: "when an occasional 'cord' has broken away altogether, when another has got loose, and turns round as the horse puts his foot on it, or when it stands up on end as the wheel touches it, the corduroy road is not pleasant to drive many miles over!" From the Northwest Angle "a beautifully decorated steamer" took the Dufferin party across the lake to Rat Portage, where settlement had just begun in 1877. At the tenting spot at Rat Portage, Lady Dufferin found that the party was "close to the house of one of our Ottawa brides, who has come out here with her husband. . . . She has one neighbor nine miles away, and a second eighteen miles off."

Meantime the Dominion government had begun to build locks around Tecamamiouen Falls, which had been known to the voyageurs as "Kettle Falls" and now began to be called "Koochiching Falls." Still later, there would be a period in the 1890's when they would be designated the "Falls of Alberton." The building of locks brought many persons to the vicinity of Fort Frances, some of whom remained even after a new government in Ottawa abandoned the project in 1878, after three years of construction, in favor of a transcontinental railroad. Although the locks, still visible at Fort Frances, never aided steamboat navigation as planned, that form of transportation remained the chief one until 1885 or thereabout for Rat Portage, until 1901 for Fort Frances, and even longer for International Falls across the river. By 1890 there were twenty-one steamboats plying between Rat Portage and Fort Frances, according to a United States timber agent who was there in that year.

These early vessels bore such picturesque names as "Lily of the West," "Couchiching," "Fleetwing," "Speedwell," "Chieftain," "Rambler," "Sunbeam," "Keewatin," "Rover,"

LADY DUFFERIN
[From her *Canadian Journal*.]

STEAMBOAT "KEENORA" ON RAINY RIVER
[Courtesy Minnesota and Ontario Paper Company.]

FORT FRANCES CANAL ABOUT 1906
[Courtesy Minnesota and Ontario Paper Company.]

"Highland Maid," "Queen," "Empress," "Thistle," "Cruiser," and "Annieac." Some of them were named for persons, like the "Victoria," "N. Mosher," "Lilly McAuley," "D. L. Mather," "Percy Sutherland," "Alma," "Mary Hatch," "Caro," and so forth. The boats won so much popular approval and became so much a part of local life that they were spoken of and regarded almost as personalities. Later there were others, whose names linger even yet in conversations heard here and there in the Rainy River country: the "Monarch," "Maple Leaf," "Agwinde," "City of Alberton," "Edma Bridges," "Shamrock," "Verbena," "Keenora," "Daisy Moore," "Swallow," and "Sir William Van Horne."

About the forms and names of these old steamboats cluster memories and emotions that defy analysis. To most residents they were the means of reaching the region; to everyone who traveled in the area they were practically the sole means of transportation between Rat Portage and the upper end of Rainy Lake, not to mention some of Rainy River's tributaries; to lonely homesteaders they were cheering sights, for they brought letters from relatives and friends, and food, clothing, provisions, and tools of all kinds; to the young and would-be young they meant moonlight rides, dances on deck, romance in all its indefinable allurement; to gold prospectors and miners they were necessary but slow conveniences; and to Indians, trappers, fishermen, and some others they became at times a substitute for canoes, for the tiny birchbark crafts and their masters were often hoisted aboard for stretches between rivers that flow into Rainy River.

Rat Portage's fortunes were tied to steamboats for a relatively short time. Late in the 1870's this former fur-trading establishment of one dwelling became, almost overnight, a town of significance on a continental railroad, the place to which machinery, rails, laborers, provisions, and timber for ties, stations, and many other purposes could be shipped. Eastward toward Port Arthur and westward toward the Rocky Mountains the shining steel of the great Canadian Pacific Railway was laid out from Rat Portage after 1879. From seven to ten sawmills were required to produce the necessary lumber for stations, warehouses, residences, and so forth; ties were cut by millions; telegraph poles were almost as numerous.

And where did the railroad find the trees for all these wooden items? There was little white or red pine in Canada west of Lake Superior, though there was plenty of cedar, tamarack, and spruce. The steamboat captains would have answered the question with precise information — and many a curse, no doubt. For they encountered drives of millions of feet of logs as they made their runs between Rat Portage and Fort Frances. Sometimes they were delayed a day or more on a run, because an immense drive from Rainy Lake, the Big Fork River, or the Little Fork was monopolizing the river and could have crushed a steamboat like an eggshell. There are records of losses of steamboats — the "Monarch," for example — from these log drives.

The Indians could have given the answer to the question, too. Theoretically they still owned a very large part of the American portion of the Rainy River basin. Since 1854 the Chippewa of Minnesota had been yielding their rights to lands north and west of Lake Superior, by treaties dated 1854, 1855, 1863, and 1866; but there was still an immense parallelogram of unceded territory stretching southwest from Rainy River, the northeast side of the rectangle. It is true that in 1866 the Bois Fort band had ceded to the United States a tract of some three thousand sections between Rainy River and Rainy Lake on the north, Vermilion River on the east, a line between

Cass Lake and the mouth of the Big Fork on the west, and the Mississippi drainage shed on the south. Within this area the Chippewa retained only two reservations: one on Nett Lake of the Little Fork drainage basin; the other, Deer Creek Reservation on the upper Big Fork. But not even the pines in this newly purchased territory were then available to lumbermen, because the land had not been surveyed nor opened to sale or homesteading. As for the timber west of the cession of 1866, theoretically there was no legal way for it to be bought and cut.

Despite the great forest fires of 1734, 1803–04, and later, there were occasional stands of magnificent white and Norway pine between the Mesabi Range on the south and Rainy River on the north, especially on the headwaters of the Big Fork and Little Fork rivers. These rivers have many tributaries, which served as drive streams for cuts of logs as far south as the sites of Chisholm, Hibbing, Virginia, and other Mesabi and Vermilion range communities. By 1890 the following Canadian mills were operating on Rainy River and Lake of the Woods, according to the report of a United States government timber agent: Fortheringham and McQuarrie, two million feet per annum; Cameron and Kenney, five million feet; Bullmen and Company, five million feet; Ross, Hall, and Brown, twelve million feet; Keewatin Lumber Company, two million feet; Western Lumber Company, twelve million feet; Dick and Banning, three and a half million feet; Hughes and Atkins, two million feet; Deserie and McDonald, nine and a half million feet; Saunders and Company, ten million feet; and Loper and Rumery, twenty-two million feet. In addition, Rat Portage had the mills of Sprague, Kendal, and Short and the Rat Portage Lumber Company. Loper and Rumery had many camps in northern Minnesota for years before the timber could be bought legally and cut. Most of the other companies got their logs from the American side of the boundary line. Some of it belonged to Indians; a vast amount was the property of the people of the United States. Eighty-five million board feet a year was not an uncommon amount to be cut on American soil and driven down to Lake of the Woods, there to be formed into great rafts and towed to Rat Portage or its suburbs, Norman and Keewatin.

As early as 1878 these depredations were reported to government agencies in Washington. On February 9 of that year John W. Jones, special timber agent at St. Paul, wrote that he had been informed that British subjects, who owned a mill at Fort Frances, "are cutting large quantities of timber from United States lands." The firm, he wrote, "has the contract for furnishing the lumber and timber for building the ship canal around the Falls of Rainy Lake River." Other reports followed, some even from Canadians, who deplored the despoiling of the public domain. In 1882, for example, W. D. Lyon of Rat Portage wrote that, "as a citizen of Canada," he thought it "really too bad to see the Country stripped of its valuable Property by the thriftless and unworthy." He added that the logs were towed to Rat Portage or shipped west by the Canadian Pacific Railway.

By 1883 the United States government was sending a special timber agent, Webster Eaton, to look over the field and report on trespasses. His account, filed in Washington, is one of many that tell the same, sad tale. Year after year one, two, or a few agents — usually only one — went over the area afoot, on snowshoes, by sleigh, or by canoe, noting all the trespasses, trying to recover damages, warning trespassers — all the while subjecting themselves to risks of being shot, of freezing to death, or of drowning. Then the illegal cutting was resumed as soon as they departed.

On July 7, 1888, N. B. Wharton reported very extensive Canadian depredations on the Bowstring and Big Fork rivers. J. S. Wallace, in 1890, wrote that in March of that year he had been to Loper and Rumery's camp, sixty-five miles west of Tower, thence on snowshoes to Rainy River and Lake of the Woods by team, and to the unceded Indian lands, where there were trespassers at various points, including one fifteen miles above the mouth of Rapid River. "Close along the boundary line," he wrote, "from Pine Creek east to Buffalo Point [*on Lake of the Woods, where in 1823 Bigsby had found the remains of a trading post*] there has been extensive trespass, but not of late years." He went on to say: "Last year I reported about eight hundred thousand feet" of trespass timber cutting, "and on this trip I learned of as much more that I did not find, thus making a million and a half last year, and I am credibly informed that in 1887–88 there was equally as much stolen. . . . Mr. David Reedy informed me that he knew men on the river who had done nothing else for the last eight years but steal timber; that one man openly boasted in his house within the last month that he had kept a certain saw mill running entirely from stolen timber."

Wallace's long letter tells so much of the region in 1890 that it is a miniature history in itself. From it one learns the names and locations of the few genuine settlers south of the border in the Rainy River basin, such as David Reedy at the mouth of the Big Fork; a man named Conners on that river; John Norquist, the sawmill owner at Roseau; O. W. Saunders, a strictly honest logger in the region, whose "sterling integrity" is mentioned with care to distinguish him from the rest; and thirteen men living illegally on the Red Lake Reservation, which then extended to Rainy River. Of these, writes Wallace, "Mr. Henry Metcalf lives at the mouth of Black River. . . . Fifteen or twenty miles west lives Edward Ward, and eighty miles farther west lives William Zippel. These three are all honest, hard-working poor men, with families of little children. When the time comes to remove the settlers from the Reservation I earnestly ask that all possible favors be shown these people, not alone because they are poor, but if they are put off there will be no place where your officers can stop on our side."

Near the southwestern end of Lake of the Woods, he reports "two little stores" at Warroad. "Along the Roseau," he continues, "from where it crosses the boundary line into Canada, for a distance of forty miles up it, there are about three hundred settlers, about fifteen hundred people; many of them from the drought stricken districts of Dakota. The country is fine agricultural land, lightly timbered with hard-wood, such as Oak and Poplar with occasional bunches of Spruce and Tamarack." They had all been pilfering timber, but only for their homestead cabins, and Wallace remarked that they were "not doing any particular harm," being "all industrious hard working people," who needed "a few boards to make them a table, a door and a bed-stead, and a floor for their log cabins." These were the pioneers who settled the western edge of the Rainy River country, mostly Scandinavians from Dakota, who, because of the flies in summer, were the only residents. It was a region at that time where "no one but a drouth stricken Dakota Swede can live," according to Wallace.

In 1892 a special timber agent of the United States estimated that the total cut of pine timber felled on the Big Fork and its tributaries since 1882 was about 85,000,000 feet; and a "detailed clerk" from the General Land Office wrote from Duluth on February 8, 1895, that trespasses on Big and Little Fork rivers and their tributaries have been a "matter of com-

mon tales and notoriety in Northern Minnesota for the last
ten or fifteen years. . . . It was common talk that the firm of
Loper and Rumly [*sic*] had a contract with the Ontario Lumber Co., of Rat Portage, Manitoba, for the delivery of one
hundred million feet of pine logs, all of which had been cut
from lands within the territory of the United States, except
about twenty million feet which is now being cut."

By that time American companies were as notorious trespassers as the Canadians, but the logs still went north to Rat
Portage. The *Rainy Lake Journal* of October 4, 1894, tells,
without mincing words or omitting names, just how the stealing on the part of American lumbering companies was accomplished, through the connivance of the auditor of the
immense county in which almost all this timber lay. Itasca
County stretched from its present southern terminus to Rainy
Lake and River on the north, for Koochiching County was
not created until 1906. Moreover, to the east, in upper St.
Louis County, there was also timber that could be, and often
was, marketed by way of Rainy River. Thus, an article
in the *Rainy Lake Journal* for July 5, 1894, estimated that
there was available at that time, "all accessible to Black bay"
on Rainy Lake, not less than two billion feet of timber. "It
is estimated," says the *Journal*, "that 700,000,000 feet of pine
is standing on Lake Vermilion and tributaries, including
Hunter's island and Kabetogama, Crane and Namekon lakes,
while on Lac La Croix and Rainy lake and tributaries there
are 1,300,000,000 feet of marketable pine."

"The method employed heretofore," the article continues,
"in logging operations in this lake and tributaries had been
to tow the logs to the falls at Fort Francis on Rainy river,
turn them over loose, and catch them in the boom near the
mouth of the river. But a river boom, and especially one in

so large a river as Rainy river, is not a safe place for storage of logs. . . . it is calculated that over 6,000,000 feet of logs already have been carried out of the boom by freshets, and scattered all over the Lake of the Woods and lost."

All this stealing of timber and marketing it through Canada came to an end shortly after 1900, for several reasons. With 1889 the United States government tried to open a large part of the unceded Indian lands to lumbermen and settlers. The Nelson Act of that year, however, proved such an abysmal failure, so far as honest operation and justice to Indians and genuine homesteaders were concerned, that the next fifteen years, more or less, were full of attempts to rectify the damage done and produce a workable law. By 1902 three million acres of land had been ceded by the Chippewa of Minnesota; 160,000 acres of timber had been sold; and 500,000 acres of arable land had been homesteaded. The United States treasury had received from these sales $1,040,440.49; and the government had paid out or advanced $2,800,000! An outraged public opinion demanded reform and an end to the pilfering of Minnesota's timber; and so the Morris Act of 1902 was passed. By 1910 nearly seven million dollars of Indians' pine had been realized from cessions; in 1917 the figure was almost nine million dollars. The whole amount of pine logged under the Morris Act until 1925 amounted to 1,321,093,198 board feet.

Another reason for the end of this lumbering era was the building of a dam at Koochiching Falls between 1905 and 1910. Still another was the construction of railroads, both common carriers and logging lines, and the development of another kind of logging operation. Then, too, there was the exhaustion of many of the great stands of white and Norway pines through illegal cutting as well as not a little legal felling.

58

THE LITTLE FORK RIVER DRIVE OF 1937
[Courtesy Minnesota and Ontario Paper Company.]

COOK SHACK IN A LUMBER CAMP
[Courtesy Zweifel-Rolleff Studio, Duluth.]

CORMORANTS ON GULL ROCK, LAKE OF THE WOODS

[Photographed by John Dobie.]

RECEPTION OF THE MARQUIS OF LORNE AT RAT PORTAGE, 1881

[From Kenora *Centennial Review*, 1936.]

A considerable factor also was the arrival of settlers after the opening of the area, between 1889 and 1902, the clearing of lands, and the growth of villages, towns, and cities.

Today Bear River Valley of the Little Fork drainage system comprises Morcom, Bearville, Carpenter, and some unorganized townships. To this area about 1890 came the first homesteader, who made use of a vacant logging camp of Loper and Rumery. About the year 1900 American companies began logging operations: Fryeberger and Stitt of Brainerd and Duluth; Backus and Brooks of Minneapolis; Shevlin, Carpenter, and Smith of Minneapolis; W. T. Bailey of Virginia on the Mesabi Iron Range, whose eight-foot camps required only three pine logs on a side; Sheldon and Mathieu of Grand Rapids; Frederick Weyerhaeuser of Iowa and Minnesota; the Engler Lumber Company of Chicago and Baudette; and others. In the fall of 1903 Backus and Brooks and Shevlin and Carpenter joined interests and organized the Namakan Lumber Company. It operated in the Bear River Valley only one season at this time, 1903–04, but much later, in 1924, when a logging railroad had been built to Thistledew Lake by a subsidiary of Backus' company, the Minnesota and Ontario Paper Company, operations were resumed. Meantime R. M. Stitt of Brainerd logged the Carpenter and West Bearville area, beginning about 1900, with headquarters near Deer Lake. His last drive went down in 1905. Other companies took their logs south to the Mississippi River or St. Louis River drainage systems. The Engler Lumber Company, however, whose mills were at Baudette, still drove the stream. Its last drive from the Bear River country was in 1917. The final drive of any timber on Bear River was in 1928.

Thus, much less than a hundred years after Graham had complained of the "eternal pines" in the borderlands, the great stands were gone. It is true that with 1910 another type of logging developed, and that cutting went on; and that logging is to this day a major industry in much of the area. The trees felled since 1928, however, have been mostly other species than white or Norway pines. The story since 1910, especially for the years from 1910 to 1928, belongs to a later chapter.

Grasses

ALL EARLY travelers on the border waters exclaimed over the unusual sight of grasses waving serenely along Rainy River. Although one and all they mention the richness of the soil, few if any of them appear to have believed that the valley would one day be an agricultural Eden. The speed with which the transformation has been made from pines and muskegs to wheat, barley, oats, potatoes, and particularly legume crops like alsike and red clover is astounding. There were few settlers between Vermilion Lake and Red River in 1890; by 1900 the old bed of Glacial Lake Agassiz was dotted here and there with straggly farms; today this is a very rich agricultural country, specializing in dairying, seed crops, certain legumes, bees, and so forth. Of course, there is still a great wilderness to draw upon, and logging continues; but the trees cut today—spruce, tamarack, cedar, scrub pine, and, preeminently, poplar—are largely those that were considered too small or unsuitable for commercial use, until pulp and paper mills were constructed.

Farms developed on the Canadian side of Rainy River a whole generation before any agricultural improvement worth mentioning occurred on the American side. The reason is not far to seek: an Indian treaty of 1873, "Number 3" in local parlance, which was the result of a spectacular and momentous gathering in the Northwest Angle, ceded the land between Lake Superior and Lake of the Woods to the Dominion and made Fort Frances the central Indian agency for the reserves on the Canadian side. Immediately farms began to appear in little clearings all the way upriver from Lake of the Woods.

Rainy River Country

These were surveyed in 1876 and twenty townships were granted free to bona fide settlers in blocks of a hundred and sixty acres per person. Each settler could purchase eighty additional acres of adjoining land at a dollar an acre, payable in three years.

In 1893 a contributor to the *Mississippi Valley Lumberman*, describing Rainy River, mentioned its "clean, high banks . . . with about six hundred farms fronting it on the Canadian side." These were served by the steamboats that developed contemporaneously and by "the River Road," still so called in the district. Running generally parallel to the river below Fort Frances, it was the chief land tie between these farms. Fort Frances was already booming as a result of the canal building from 1875 to 1878, the emigration trade of the Dawson Route, commercial fishing, and logging operations. It was, also, still a fur-trading post of the Hudson's Bay Company.

On October 7, 1874, fire broke out in the fort and destroyed some of the buildings, which were very old and huddled together. The destroyed structures were replaced, and the fort continued as a trading post until the season of 1897–98. By that time the village of Fort Frances and the surrounding settlements were growing so fast that it was no longer feasible to carry on a fur-trading business. The post became a sale shop only and continued as such until it was destroyed by fire on February 2, 1903.

Joseph Biddison, an early resident of Fort Frances, recalls in his manuscript reminiscences how the old post looked in his childhood and youth. His father, Daniel Biddison, had come from England in the 1870's as an engineer of the "Louise Thompson," which carried supplies across Rainy Lake to the canal construction. He had brought his wife and seven children from Birmingham to a log house, twenty-four feet square, that he had erected on the "River Range" and insulated with birchbark; and he had cleared his land in the long winters, when the "Louise Thompson" and his later boats for the run to Rat Portage were frozen up. In such an atmosphere Joseph grew up, in the little hamlet whose life centered about the old post, "located just south of the Paper Company's substation about 100 feet from the river bank." It was a very picturesque location, he adds. "One could see Koochiching falls and look downriver for a distance of nearly two miles. The falls were a magnificent sight throughout the year. On certain days the roar of the falls could be heard for eight or nine miles. Some of the old residents maintained that the variations in the sound of the rushing water indicated the kind of weather in prospect for the following 24-hour period. The Hudson's Bay Fort and the buildings occupied slightly more than an acre of ground which was enclosed by a palisade made of tamarac poles, peeled and sharpened at the top. The poles or posts were about ten feet high."

An American taxidermist of Warren, Minnesota, journeyed up and down Rainy River a good deal between the years 1889 and 1901, keeping a diary at all times. This young man, Ernest L. Brown, was deeply interested in wild life, and to get the specimens he wanted and to secure competent guides for his trips, he made friends with the Indians. His diaries, therefore, are replete with data on the natives and on the countryside. Often a passenger on the steamboats, he mentions their names, describes his fellow travelers, and even tells of the farms where he stopped overnight, when he journeyed by canoe or small boat. Hugh Kerr's home was not far from Fort Frances; the Shortreads lived just above Manitou Rapids; and old Michel Morrison, after fifteen years of dog-sled travel via the Northwest Angle carrying the mail between Fort Frances and the one house that then was Rat Portage, not to mention eight years' service with the Hudson's Bay Company, had his residence at the mouth of Rainy River. George McPherson was on Lake of the Woods, probably on the site of Kenora. On the American side of the river there were Alexander Baker, the "old hermit," on the site of International Falls; Thomas McKinstry at the mouth of the Little Fork; David Reedy at the mouth of the Big Fork; and, on down the river, the Petersons, Wilson, Andrew Hunter and "his squaw," George Sinclair, George Holly, and Lee Moffett. On the south shore of Lake of the Woods were William Zippel, Alonzo Wheeler, a man named Griffith, Ole and Prosser's fishery near Zippel's, and Hans Osmus at Long Point. Brown also mentions the hamlets of Emo and Rainy River, originally called Beaver Mills. Most of the earliest settlers of the region gained a livelihood, in part at least, from the trap line or with the gun.

Brown in his diaries probably represents the region more accurately than anyone else has succeeded in depicting it for the period of early settlement on the American side. According to him, the chief concentrations of Indians were at Black Bay of Rainy Lake, on Lake Kabetogama, along the Vermilion River to Tower, on Nett Lake, at Manitou Rapids, at the narrows of Bowstring River, on the upper Big Fork, on the Canadian side of the outlet of Rainy Lake, at the mouth of Rainy River, at the Sault Rapids on Rainy River below the Manitou whitewater, at Warroad, about Red Lake, and at various places on Lake of the Woods, particularly at Rocky Point, Long Point, and Buffalo Point. He even supplies the Indian names for the chief men among the Chippewa. They offer an odd assortment: Shonia Geshik, Maybombe, Mache-

beness, Nemeshobeness, Mickinock, Waubanogut, Boscocog-
gin, King Billy, or Lashashagishigoka, chief man of the Black
Bay band, and many others.

These natives and their followers and families were still
practicing their age-old customs, such as dancing, gathering
birchbark for canoes, offering prayers to the spirits of bear,
moose, caribou, beaver, otter, and other animals before going
on a hunt, building their fish traps on rivers, having dog feasts,
playing their ancient gambling and other games, smoking their
pipes, celebrating New Year's Day in French fashion, and
otherwise living and acting as their ancestors had done for
centuries. Brown moved among them as an equal and thus
had opportunity to note how the Chippewa of the Rainy
River country lived in the last decade of the nineteenth century.

Brown also was an uncommonly astute observer of wild
life. Few regions have been so carefully examined in this re-
spect for birds and mammals, before settlement got under way,
by one well versed in ornithology and biology. Time and
again his diaries record trips of weeks' duration into swamp-
lands, up and down Rainy River and all its tributaries, all
about and across Lake of the Woods, into the region of rocky
grandeur and infinite lakes between Fort Frances and Rat
Portage, north of Rainy Lake, west of big Vermilion Lake,
and over the muskegs and swamps near Red Lake. Every day
he recorded minutely the birds he saw, the nests he found,
and the effect of forest and prairie songs on his ear and
spirit. With Indians for guides he stalked the moose, caribou,
elk, deer, bear, wolverine, fisher, and other mammals. His
descriptions of caribou hunts in swirling snow, across frozen
lakes, are worth the time of any lover of wild life; and the
dogged persistence with which he pursued a certain big elk

one year is amusing as well as indicative of the kind of sport still available in the Rainy River country in the 1890's. One winter he spent on the trap line on the headwaters of the Big Fork, and his diary describes how he and two companions built the trapping shack, how they ate and slept, how they set and picked up traps, and what he saw and heard in the heart of the continental wilderness. He also cruised for pine timber and prospected for gold; and thus he covered the area from north to south and from east to west as it probably never was studied before and probably never will be again by one individual. The distinguished ornithologists and the rich sportsmen looking for game, whom he guided at times, were more fortunate than they probably realized.

By 1890 sportsmen and tourists were beginning to appear. Indeed, Rat Portage had developed a considerable tourist trade as soon as the Canadian Pacific ran trains on regular schedules. For fifteen years or more it was the metropolis for this region, with tourists, sportsmen, cruisers, gold prospectors, and fishermen making it their gateway for entering and leaving, for getting supplies, and for sending out lumber, fish, and other freight.

One of the early tourists was a young man who was to become in later years a distinguished member of the Minneapolis bar, Edward C. Gale. In 1890 he traveled by rail to Rat Portage and thence by steamer to Fort Frances. A little later he published an account of what he saw and experienced, especially the unusual sights and activities that he viewed from the "Chieftain" as it steamed upriver, commanded by a "Guernseyan corsair." Gale's description of how vessels got through the rapids is the answer to many modern questioners concerning this obviously difficult part of the navigation. "Both rapids are quite swift," he wrote, "and it is generally

POUND NET, LAKE OF THE WOODS
[Courtesy Minnesota Department of Conservation.]

GILL NET, LAKE OF THE WOODS
[Courtesy Minnesota Department of Conservation.]

A GILL NET REEL

[Courtesy Minnesota Department of Conservation.]

RAISING A POUND NET

[Courtesy Minnesota Department of Conservation.]

the practice of the boats to take on a special pilot and fasten
hawsers to the boat a quarter of a mile long, running up
stream, for the Indians and the passengers to pull on by way
of assisting the craft over the rapids. It is naturally a time of
great excitement." On this trip of 1890 "the Indian pilot became fairly frantic; the Guernseyan corsair volleyed forth
his most brilliant oaths, and we and the Indians at the hawsers
. . . pulled so hard as to fairly snap the boat out of the jaws
of Scylla and Charybdis and project ourselves at the same
time into some neighboring gooseberry bushes."

Brown gives a little more information about the means for
surmounting the difficult rapids. Recounting a trip in 1891
on the "Shamrock," which pulled a barge loaded with cattle,
he writes: "At the Soo rapids We all got out to walk while
they got out the tow line   got all the Indians ahold to help
over the rapids. The Manitou not so long but terrible swift,"
and the crew "had to tie a long line to a post across the river
and wind up by hand on the capstan   took about an hour of
hard work." It may be added here that remains of the capstan
are still to be seen on the American side of the rapids.

Commercial fishing became an industry very early. On his
first trips about the countryside Brown mentions fishermen,
especially those on the south shore of Lake of the Woods, Ole
and Prosser, and "Old German Hans." On October 25, 1894,
a Rat Portage correspondent of the *Nor'Wester* of Winnipeg
was quoted as saying: "Fish is king here just now and it makes
one feel very wealthy to watch the loading of these cars
with such splendid samples of the finny tribe and to realize
something of the enormous food supplies which are the common heritage of Canada. Of course the fish we see do not
belong to us; they are caught in the American waters of the
lake, and are landed here in bond; so that we are not per-

mitted to purchase them at any price." It was at this time that caviar, or sturgeon roe, began to make Lake of the Woods famous among gourmets.

That same year another local newspaper reported the names, owners, and locations of the several fishing stations on Rainy River and Lake of the Woods: "The Reid fishing station at the mouth of the Rainy river, operated by the Baltimore Fish Co., employs over eighty men. The Sandusky Fishing Co. also operates extensively on the Rainy river and the product of these fisheries runs up well into the thousands in value. The companies mentioned operate their own tugs and ship their product to the American cities by way of Rat Portage and the Canadian Pacific Railway." And a new firm was just beginning operations: "H. E. Finske & Co., who for several weeks have been prospecting for fishing grounds in this section, have finally located at Crane lake, where they have established their headquarters. Buildings are now in course of construction for a general supply store and later on ice houses, warehouses, etc., will be erected. It is the intention of the company to expend about $10,000 this year on this station. The product will be shipped to the various markets by way of Tower. A regular freight line will be established between Crane lake and Tower to facilitate the handling of the product and by which all supplies will be brought in. About twenty men will be employed and the catch will consist principally of sturgeon, pike and pickerel." Thus, in 1894, a new transportation route was threatening the supremacy of Rat Portage in this field. To a considerable extent it succeeded, as we shall see, though the difficulties surmounted in carrying one person or one ton of freight between Rainy Lake and the end of rails at Tower were as great as ever they had been on the Dawson Route. The region's unique transportation methods entitle it to a high place in the history of the world's unusual routes of travel.

Rat Portage was having more serious problems, however. From 1870 to 1884 both Manitoba and Ontario claimed jurisdiction over the area between Lake Superior and Lake of the Woods. A commission was appointed in 1878 to arbitrate the matter, but the Dominion parliament refused to ratify its recommendation. In 1881 Parliament passed an act which made the disputed territory a part of Manitoba. Ontario officials already in possession of offices refused to budge. In September, 1883, an election occurred, which chose members to both provincial legislatures. Finally, the question was taken before the Privy Council of England, where it was settled in 1884 in favor of Ontario. Meantime Rat Portage was growing. In 1885 it had a population of 720, and there were 4,564 inhabitants of the district in which it was located. The latter figure had increased to 10,369 by 1901 and to 15,490 by 1911; in 1950 Kenora alone had about 8,700 residents. Rat Portage was incorporated as a Manitoba town in 1882, as an Ontario township in 1883, and as a city in 1892. Its name was changed to Kenora about 1899.

To the south the Sandridge Trail along the fourth, or Campbell, beach of Glacial Lake Agassiz was witnessing the first waves of a mass migration that would be the final wash of the American frontier of settlement. The government timber agent of 1890 wrote of some fifteen hundred persons in the Roseau Valley in northwestern Minnesota, especially of the "drought-stricken" Scandinavians from the Dakotas. Over the great natural highway creaked covered wagons, as they had rolled through forests and over plains for a hundred years and more to people North America. By 1895 the population in the northeastern part of Kittson County was suffi-

ciently large for a division. The new unit was named Roseau
County after the stream so prominent in local history since
La Vérendrye's time. Its county seat bears the same name,
though at first the little settlement was known as Jadis.
Brown's diaries are full of references to Jadis, to the Scandi-
navian settlers with whom he stayed overnight on his long
stage journeys from Warren to Warroad, and to a hostelry of
local fame, erected by Roswell Waterman in 1887 on the
river bank half a mile north of the present town of Roseau.
"Waterman's" was a haven of rest and repose, as well as of
good food, to those who traveled the Sandridge Trail. In
1895 a flour mill was built and the village of Roseau was
platted. The state census of that year lists both Jadis and
Roseau, giving them a combined population of 474 inhabitants. Reed canary grass, from which the river, village, and
county get their names, still grows wild in the bottom lands
of the former Roseau Lake, where the Hudson's Bay Company had a trading post as late as 1849.

Warroad also began to develop about 1890. There had
been an Indian village there since La Vérendrye's day, at
least, and John Tanner's story is intimately connected with
it. The village of Badger was platted in 1895, named after
that odd creature, which, according to Brown, digs the bur-
rows and holes for most of the wild inhabitants of this region.
Other villages that came into existence at this time were Pelan,
Greenbush, and Salol.

North and northwest of Roseau County, across the international line, still another type of settlement was in progress.
In August, 1877, Lady Dufferin visited this area before proceeding to the Northwest Angle, where we have already seen
her, bumping over the corduroys of the Dawson Trail and
relishing thereafter the ease of a gaily decorated steamer

crossing Lake of the Woods to the nascent village of Rat Portage. She was deeply impressed with the Mennonites and the farms they had carved out of an inhospitable prairie during the three years since their arrival from Russia; and she had many good words for these "hard-working, honest, sober, simple, hardy people."

Gold

THE QUIET of the border's idyllic life was shattered by the discovery of gold, first near Rat Portage, later on Rainy Lake. Accounts differ as to the time and place of discovery. It is tradition in Kenora that Captain Walpole Roland, on one of the surveying parties for the Canadian Pacific, noted the presence of the glittering metal near Lake of the Woods. Another version of the discovery legend is that even earlier, in 1875, George Stuntz was sent to Loon Lake, just east of Rainy Lake, to examine a reported discovery of gold there. Earlier still, in 1865, occurred the so-called "Vermilion Gold Rush," when hundreds of hurrying feet passed over the Mesabi Iron Range going north to prospect around Vermilion Lake. Although a great industrial development mushroomed there and died almost as rapidly, the owners of some of those speeding feet, including Stuntz, saw evidences of iron and remembered them. Years later, recollections of those gold-rush days brought about the opening of the greatest open-pit iron mines in the world about a hundred miles south of Rainy Lake.

There was, then, ample tradition regarding the presence of precious metals on the border. Beginnings of actual mining in the neighborhood of Rat Portage were unspectacular, but by 1894 the proprietor of the Russell House in that village was advertising his hotel and region by listing on his card some thirty mines, distant from three to twenty-two miles from Rat Portage. As usual in gold-mining areas, no lack of imagination was displayed in naming these now-forgotten mines. They ran the gamut, from the "Queen of Sheba" to the "Woodchuck," with the "Minerva," the "King," the "Sultana," the "Rajah," and the "Mikado" satisfying the obvious interest in royalty, and the "Dead Broke" and the "Black Jack" testifying to other propensities of the owners.

As time went on, new discoveries north of Kenora moved the focus of attention from Lake of the Woods to the region of Red Lake, Trout Lake, Stanley Lake, and the Pickle Crow area, but Kenora remained the center of these operations for an area extending two hundred miles to the north and east, as well as for the older mining area. Today in Kenora one hears much of this northern gold-mining region, which is served largely by aircraft.

There was no lack of the spectacular at Rainy Lake, on the other hand. One evening in July, 1893, George W. Davis reached Little American Island in that lake, spent the night alone there, and in the morning panned some quartz and found gold. The news spread so quickly that by 1894 there was no dearth of mines, prospectors, or mining camps. The most publicized mine was the Little American, owned by a Duluth group calling itself the Bevier Mining and Milling Company. Operations were in full swing in 1894, with a new village on Black Bay, a five-stamp mill, a newspaper, and the usual concomitants of mining-camp life. Other mines soon discovered and opened were Big American on Dryweed Island, Wiegand's, Lucky Coon, Little Canada, Wiggins, Mastodon, Joe La Course, Red Gut, Alice A., Lucella, Madelaine, Lyle, and others. Some of these were on the American side of the lake, but the majority were on the Canadian, especially on Seine River. According to Horace Johnson, long president of the Duluth and Iron Range Rail Road Company and therefore closely associated with the supply of men and material to these new camps, the American operations "did not amount to much, but the gold fields near Mine Center on Shoal Lake and

Rainy River Country

Bad Vermilion were the productive mines." Nevertheless, one hears almost nothing today about these successful ventures, whereas one cannot be on or about Rainy Lake for more than a few hours without being told at least one story about Gold Harbor or Holman mines or the diggings on Bushy Head Island or Little American Mine, particularly the last. The explanation lies in Rainy Lake City.

That community sprang into existence overnight. It was incorporated on May 17, 1894, by the Rainy Lake Improvement Company of Duluth, and a photograph of that period shows it as a clutter of tents, log houses, tar-paper shacks, and covered wagons. By early summer it had a population of nearly four hundred, which shortly rose to five hundred or thereabout, before the inevitable decline set in. It boasted, according to its newspaper, the *Rainy Lake Journal,* "three general stores, a hardware store, 3 hotels, a barber shop, two restaurants, a post office, customs office and 5 saloons." Of these enterprises the butcher shop was the only one independent of outside supply, for, according to the recollections of one of the residents, "its stock in trade consisted principally of moose, caribou, and venison." An entire moose carcass sold for five dollars, a caribou for two dollars, and a deer for a dollar. Whitefish, pike, and pickerel were sold for five cents apiece.

Outside supply — transportation, in other words — was the great problem. The machinery for the mines, the sawmill that soon developed, and the steamboats that shortly appeared on Crane Lake and Rainy Lake, came in by way of Tower, the Vermilion Iron Range village at the end of the Duluth and Iron Range Railroad. Horace Johnson of that railroad years later dug up in the archives of his company the story of the fantastic operations that ensued. A portage trail was cut from Tower on Vermilion Lake to Harding on Crane Lake, where

74

a community developed around Finske's Iron Fish Company's plant, the customs house, and the post office. From Tower the machinery, goods, and passengers were carried by steamboat to the Vermilion dam, where the trail began. Twenty-six miles of corduroy, gumbo, mire, rocks, and holes — optimistically called a road — ensued. At Harding another steamboat waited to carry freight and passengers to Kettle Falls at the east end of Rainy Lake. There, after another transfer, the weary traveler, now two days out from Tower, found another vessel waiting to take him to the mines on Rainy Lake. Today by car one covers this entire distance between a late lunch and an early dinner.

Something of the agony of that trip can be glimpsed by reading the local editor's comments just after he had completed a trip in August, 1894: "The trip via Duluth, Port Arthur and Rat Portage, is a long and tedious one. And travelling over the Tower route, while confined to only two days' travel, is something to dread, on account of the long, dreary and tiresome ride over the twenty-six mile portage between Lake Vermilion and Crane lake." The worst stretch began "about three miles out from Everett's landing at Crane lake. The country there is low with springs, and the road there is now worn into a perfect mudhole, with no bottom, except piles of rock." The "buckboard" advertised by the owners of this luxurious transportation system was "a common lumber wagon, with oak planks stretched across the bolsters, to which is attached iron supports for ordinary wagon seats, not guilty of spring or cushion, with no side-boards to hold babies or baggage from dropping to the ground: in fact the loss of baggage, and an occasional baby, is of everyday occurrence." In contrast, the little steamboats — the "Libby" on Vermilion Lake, the "May Carter" on Crane Lake, and the "Walter S.

Lloyd" on Rainy Lake — were safe and comfortable, "and the owners and officers of the boats try to make the journey pleasant to their passengers."

Johnson tells of five thousand dollars spent on this "road" in 1895 in an endeavor to improve it, which resulted in filling the tracks at Tower with carloads of machinery. "Nothing was done in 1896," he says, "but in 1897 the Golden Star, a mine on Bad Vermilion, started operating and in 1898 more machinery was received for this mine"; and so another five thousand dollars was spent on the so-called road. He adds that "most of the men, up to 1897 and 1898, went via Winnipeg and by boat through Lake of the Woods and Rainy Lake, except in the winter, when all the men went through Tower." After the improvements of 1897 men could take the Tower route even in summer. According to Johnson, there were "fifteen and more teams on the road all the time. . . . Mail was hauled through Tower for all points north, including Ft. Frances, Ranier, and what is now International Falls and the mining centers."

Life in Rainy Lake City, the metropolis for all this mining activity, was never humdrum. Prospectors came by scores on every steamboat from Rat Portage or Tower. Some of them were important men, like Horace V. Winchell, who had been coming to the region ever since 1887, when he had made a geological survey of it for Minnesota. His long description of his canoe trips that summer was printed at once and is still used by geologists and others interested in the geology, geography, and natural history of the area. Oddly enough, he reported, and apparently observed, no evidences of gold at that time, though he stresses the abundance of quartz veins, so obvious to anyone. When prospectors sought gold in these rocks, it was always veins of quartz that they followed as signposts.

Gold

All about the countryside canoed little groups of men, secretively trying out this boulder or that ledge with their hammers. Even Brown, the peripatetic taxidermist and diary-keeper, turned prospector. For once we have a diary kept by one of this usually voiceless class of men. Although his trip into the Manitou Lake country showed up no lode of gold, it was not time lost, since the beauty and grandeur of the scenery appear to have been adequate compensation for Brown, the nature lover.

Everyone, in fact, turned prospector. A correspondent to an Ashtabula, Ohio, newspaper wrote: "I struck the city at this time. Went to get shaved. There was no barber in town. All were out prospecting. Then I wished to see the postmaster. I asked for him; he was prospecting. So I returned to my hotel, the Lake Shore House. The proprietor had gone prospecting. So it went, from the genial banker, Mr. Butler, and the editor of the *Rainy Lake Journal*, down to the mechanic and day laborer."

Rainy Lake City had the usual floating population of mining camps. Some of them were worthy of Virginia City, Last Chance Gulch, and Prickly Pear Diggings. As ever, most of them went armed and were proficient in ballistics. For instance, the village bar fly, "Patty the Bird," was out in the open spaces one day, congratulating himself that here he might enjoy unmolested the contents of a large whisky bottle. Suddenly his gurgles were interrupted by splintering glass, as the bottle neck broke into many pieces. It was observed that a practical joker, who had recently shot off the bail of a pail of water carried by John Fransen, was standing not far off, his forty-five still smoking. It was also observed that his grin showed satisfaction with his excellent marksmanship.

"Gold Bug Jimmie," on the other hand, was not nearly so

sure of himself. He loved to prospect, but on every venture into the ubiquitous forests he became lost. After several rescues, he decided to blaze his outward trail in the manner advocated by his wilderness-wise friends and acquaintances. On his next trip, therefore, he carefully blazed tree after tree, making a good gash on its face as he advanced. Lost again, he was rescued, and when he complained that the system advocated by the cruisers and experienced woodsmen had brought no better results than before, he was gently informed that he had cut the blazes on the wrong sides of the trees.

Another six-shooting artist turned up in a saloon in Rainy Lake City. Being in the money at the moment, he gave the saloonkeeper a bill of some size in payment for his drink. The proprietor rang up the money but gave the customer no change. The latter remonstrated, but to no avail. When argument seemed futile, he hauled out his trusty weapon, and with "Well, I'll ring it up for you then," he emptied its contents into the cash register. The speed with which he got his change was noticeable, the other customers remarked.

Sanitary conditions in Rainy Lake City left something to be desired in those gay days of the 'nineties. When a typhoid fever epidemic broke out in the summer of 1894, no doctor had as yet appeared in the "city." Therefore a former Civil War army surgeon's assistant, one "Doc" Lewis, took charge, and with liberal doses of quinine and whisky checked the spread of the disease, or so it is related.

Rainy Lake City lasted until 1901. In 1906 one person was resident in it. The Gold Harbor and Holman mines, about a mile and a half east of Rainy Lake City, did not run after 1894, but Bushy Head, under the management of "Bushy Head" Johnson, managed to persist for two years. Operations at the most important American mine, the Little American, fluctuated, and management changed hands, but it survived until 1901. Johnson writes that "Operations slowed down and ceased entirely in 1901," though, he adds in parentheses, writing in 1926, "Some mines in this section are working again." The Little American was one of those for which resuscitation was attempted in the 1920's and again in the middle 1930's, but today the timbered shaft, the broken windlass, and the diamond-drill cores all about the pile of tailings on the little rocky island are picturesque reminders of a vanished splendor. A witticism in International Falls runs to this effect: "Our city is unique; it is paved with gold." That is literally true, for at one muddy stage in its career, the city mixed the resplendent tailings from Little American with the less stable elements of its streets.

How much else International Falls owes to the Little American is hard to evaluate. Perhaps its very existence. Brown's "old hermit," Alexander Baker, had been living close to Koochiching Falls for several years when Winchell passed through on his surveying trip in 1887. Baker is generally accorded the honor of the title, "founder of International Falls," the city that now occupies the site of Borup's trading post. A plaque and a grade school named for Baker keep his memory green in that place. He may have been the first to perceive the potential value of the falls, though his prospecting record in other regions suggests that his original interest was mining. About 1872 he turned up at the falls and squatted there, for as yet the land was unsurveyed. After government surveyors had been through in 1880, he filed a homestead claim in 1883 and secured the patent for his 163½ acres on December 30, 1884. There the state census marshal of 1895 found him four years before his death and recorded that he was then seventy years of age, had been born in Scotland, had been a resident of Min-

nesota for thirty years, and had been a resident of the enu-
meration district for twenty-three years. Tradition has it that
he came from Drumarcher, Scotland, to the United States at
the age of twenty-three in an endeavor to find his elder
brother. When that mission proved futile, he remained in the
country, served as a sailor under Farragut in the Civil War,
had steamboat experience on the Mississippi, and prospected
for a copper-mining company on the north shore of Lake Superior. The census, however, records him as a veteran "sol-
dier," and gives his occupation as "miner."

It is difficult, therefore, to state whether the first resident's
choice of location was based on interest in the potential water
power of the falls or on proximity to possible mining locations. In either event, closeness to an established center of
Britishers like himself doubtless played an important part in
his choice. Fort Frances was enjoying the Dawson Trail boom
about the time of his advent. In any case, neither he nor Fort
Frances did anything about the waterpower development until a trained eye had seen it. Winchell saw its possibilities at once,
and for four years he tried to get an option on Baker's land.
Finally, in 1891, he secured a year's lease. In 1892 Baker's
land was purchased for six thousand dollars by the company
that Winchell had organized in Minneapolis. This townsite
company took its own name from the old Indian word for the
region about the falls, "Koochiching," and gave it also to the
townsite, which the new company now boomed. C. J. Rockwood was a member of the company, and his intention from
the start was to develop waterpower for making paper.

Just how much success Rockwood and the Koochiching
Company would have had without the gold rush, however, is
problematical; for it was the discovery of gold that probably
made the townsite venture a success. On the other hand, it is

apparent that settlement of the general area was inevitable at this time. The November 8, 1894, issue of the *Rainy Lake Journal* scored the General Land Office for failing to survey the region on the river beyond Koochiching, intimating that the rich lumberman could get townships surveyed wherever and whenever he wanted to log them, whereas the poor, average homesteader had no chance to get a new home. Thus it is obvious that pressure for homesteads was great at the moment. This conjecture is borne out by another statement in the same newspaper article: "Several hundred settlers have squatted on the lands along the Rainy river and tributaries this year and not a foot of the land is yet surveyed." On July 5, 1894, the paper mentioned the "new town" of Hannaford "at the mouth of the Big Fork," with its sawmill "ready to begin operations, a good store . . . and a large hotel." It adds that "settlers are going into the Big Fork and Black river country at a great rate and that it will not be long before the best claims there are all taken up." The issue of October 25 of the same year tells of "a large number of settlers" who had gone to the Little Fork Valley "this year," and of "a few settlers" that had "located this year in the Rat Root valley." Thus there might have been a settlement on the American side of the falls without any other reason than pressure of homesteaders. It is certain, however, that Rainy Lake City, twelve miles east of Koochiching, was in no way a detriment to the building up of the new townsite.

The first issue of the *Rainy Lake Journal*, which appeared on June 28, 1894, contains a long article entitled "Koochiching: The Promising New Town Just Started at the Falls of Alberton. Only Two Weeks Old, But a Hummer." The location is described as "ideal" for a city, "nearly level, sloping gently on three sides to the Rainy river," with "the picturesque falls of Alberton" directly in front of the town, "where the mighty volume of water in the Rainy river plunges down a 25-foot precipice, affording a water power unsurpassed on the American continent."

Through columns of the Rainy Lake City newspaper one can watch the lusty infant grow. By July 26, Curly Bedford was building for himself a neat log house on "Second street west of Second Avenue east," an address which shows how complicated the street gridironing was becoming; A. W. Mertens was moving his family into his recently completed "residence"; "the pioneer resident of Koochiching, Alex. Baker," was making a trip to Duluth, or, as expressed in a later issue, "to the outside world"; and the "Highland Maid's" recent cargo of lumber from Rat Portage was being made into a building, characteristically housing a hotel and a saloon.

By August 9 the "humming" mentioned in the first issue of the newspaper was getting louder. "Koochiching is less than two months old and to-day there are four frame and four log buildings, sixteen tents used for business and residence purposes, two general stores, a hardware store, a lumber yard, a wholesale liquor and wholesale cigar store," and "a railroad is only a question of a short time."

So thought the junior editor in August, 1894. So, presumably, thought Rockwood of the townsite company, now busily selling lots to new residents. By the end of that year Rockwood was a wiser man, for he had gone to New York in an endeavor to interest John D. Rockefeller in the waterpower development of Koochiching, which of course would mean also a railroad to the place. The oil magnate, flushed with his recent triumph over the Merritts, the "Seven Iron Men" of the Mesabi, and now owning not only their fabulously rich iron mines but also their new railroad, which terminated only

82

RANIER ABOUT 1905
[Courtesy Minnesota and Ontario Paper Company.]

RAINY LAKE CITY, 1894
[Courtesy Minnesota and Ontario Paper Company.]

KOOCHICHING FALLS IN THE EARLY 1900's
[Courtesy Minnesota and Ontario Paper Company.]

a hundred miles south of Koochiching, blandly refused even to see Rockwood, much less promise to build his railroad north a hundred miles from Virginia.

Disillusioned but still hopeful, Rockwood next tried the great Saginaw lumber company of Wright, Davis, and Company, which had extensive timberlands in northern Minnesota; and he even got from that company in 1898 a tentative contract to run its logging railroad north from the Hibbing terminus to Koochiching. But fate intervened in the person of the Empire Builder, James J. Hill. Early in 1899 he bought the Wright, Davis logging railroad when he purchased the timberlands for their iron ore contents. Thus Hill gleefully reached his objective of outwitting Rockefeller, but Koochiching and its townsite owners were sad.

Still another evidence of the interest of Big Business in northern Minnesota and adjacent Ontario projects in the closing years of the nineteenth century is the fact that Rockwood almost succeeded in getting a new Canadian railroad to include Koochiching and Duluth on its line. Premier Thomas Greenway of Manitoba was willing, at first, but William McKenzie of the firm of McKenzie and Mann, which got the contract eventually, induced "Mr. Greenway to visit Toronto and the result is spiked to the ties from Port Arthur to Winnipeg and a thousand miles or more beyond," to quote Rockwood. In other words, a railroad was built west from Port Arthur, but it touched Fort Frances and not Koochiching on its way to Winnipeg and out on the prairies. Thus Fort Frances got quick access to "the outside world" when this Canadian Northern Railway reached it in 1901; but several more years were to elapse before its neighbor across the falls had railroad connections with the same, much-desired objective.

Rainy River Country

Thus Fort Frances was still in the lead, and so were the little Canadian communities up and down Rainy River, for transportation needs were filled through Canadian outlets. The village of Fort Frances, Ontario, was incorporated on April 3, 1903, but there had been formal government in that place since May 30, 1891, when the municipality of Alberton, comprising the hamlet of Fort Frances and the townships of McIrvine, Roddick, and Crozier, had been established. In 1898 Fort Frances and McIrvine withdrew from Alberton, which reorganized on April 9, 1898. After 1903 began the modern development of Fort Frances, the oldest settlement of continued existence beyond Lake Superior, which, as Fort St. Pierre, the North West Company's fort, the X Y Company's fort, the Hudson's Bay Company's post, Fort Frances the trading post, and now Fort Frances the village and city, had been in existence since 1731. How far its modern development would have gone without the assistance of its neighbor across the waterfall it is impossible to say. Both waited for someone with money and vision to develop their greatest common asset, Koochiching Falls.

Meantime the river villages became sawmill communities, paying tribute to both Fort Frances and Rat Portage as their transportation centers. O'Leary, referring to a sawmill in Fort Frances, seen on his trip in 1874, prophesied that "the American civilizer," as he termed it, meant the coming of civilization. Other mills followed this one, which had been erected by H. S. Fowler in 1873. As the lumbering industry worked down-river, sawmills were established at Spooner, Baudette, Rainy River, Clementson, and Emo. The Rainy River Boom Company had its boom just above the town of Rainy River, Ontario. There the logs for various mills were sorted and boomed. The *Mississippi Valley Lumberman* of August 11,

1893, after describing the new town of Hannaford, adds: "At this place the Canadian lumbermen have built a boom to hold logs that formerly went to the mouth of Rainy river to be rafted. It is rumored that the seven mill companies at Rat Portage intend moving their mills up there, and will barge their lumber across Lake of the Woods instead of towing logs in rafts, as an average loss of about 20 per cent will be saved, besides the difference in cost of towing."

In 1904 still another boom company was formed. It was called the International Boom Company, it had Minnesota men as officers, and it was capitalized at $50,000. Thomas H. Shevlin was president, E. L. Carpenter vice-president, G. S. Eddy secretary, and William L. Brooks treasurer. Edward W. Backus, James A. Mathieu, and G. S. Parker were directors. These names probably meant little as yet to residents of Koochiching and Fort Frances, but soon both communities, and Kenora as well, would count their owners, especially Backus and Brooks, as saviors of a sort. The formation of the company also serves to show that, though the Canadian side of the river was ceasing to depend on river transportation of logs, the American side must still resort to booms and rafts. This also was the time when the Morris Act was beginning to function, ending the theft of timber in northern Minnesota and so depriving Rat Portage of much of its business.

The operation of the Morris Act and its immediate precursors also meant the speedy opening of the south bank of the river to homesteaders. The final rush of settlers now built up Littlefork, Loman, Spooner, Baudette, and other communities, some of which had had a precarious sort of existence for a decade or so. The state census of 1895 shows how few were the settlers in that year. Koochiching is credited with a hundred and twenty-eight inhabitants; Ray is listed, but it appears not to have been the modern community of that name, but one closer to Koochiching; Reedy, at the mouth of the Little Fork, is included, among whose residents is listed Thomas McKinstry, an Irish farmer who had lived there for eighteen years; and there were scattered groups about the rest of that part of Itasca County now known as Koochiching County. Not until 1906 did Koochiching County succeed in establishing itself as a separate government unit, and then only after a spectacular fight with its parent county. How recent the development of Lake of the Woods County has been is shown by the fact that it was carved from Beltrami County in 1922.

Littlefork, the village, is one word, whereas the river is always spelled as two words. At a great bend in the river, settlement started in 1902, though a slight beginning may have been made in 1899. White and Street, a townsite company, platted the spot into four blocks in 1901, and residents began to appear the following year. There the inevitable sawmill appeared in 1902, and a newspaper was begun in 1903. A Rainy River steamboat, the "Welcome," added the Little Fork run to its schedule in 1902. Occasionally, too, when water conditions were right, the "Itasca," built and launched at Baudette, also ascended the Little Fork. This boat was the first of the Northern Navigation Company's vessels and it operated on both the Rainy and the Little Fork after 1903. Another of the company's boats, the "Seamo," was the "Mud Hen" in local parlance. The "Sea Gull," a third vessel, operated exclusively on Rainy Lake.

Many of the pioneers of Littlefork and its hinterland are still living there or in the state, and they remember vividly the rigorous conditions under which they carved their homes from the wilderness of forest. With a slight change here and there, their experiences might easily have been those of the squirrel hunters of the Ohio Valley a hundred years earlier. There was the same difficulty of access; a similar period of primitive existence lasted until a log house could be erected; forest trees were felled with the same, back-breaking labor; and markets, post offices, and neighbors were almost as far away in Minnesota as they had been in the Ohio Valley. Frontier conditions, however, prevailed only five years at most in Littlefork, for a railroad reached the place in 1907. Steamboats on the rivers and pioneering vanished simultaneously.

Thus the years from 1905 to 1910 may be taken to stand, in general, for the end of a period in the Rainy River country. In those five years two important events happened which were to mark the beginning of a new era. The development of waterpower at Koochiching Falls began; and two railroads linked the border with the rest of the United States.

ℬ. 𝒟. and 𝒜. 𝒟.

ALL HISTORY in the borderlands about Rainy Lake is divided into two eras: B. D., or Before the Dam; and A. D., After the Dam. The building of the great structure, between 1905 and 1910, has altered the course of events and conditions in the whole region between Rainy Lake and Lake of the Woods more than any other single factor.

Having been disappointed by three representatives of Big Business, the Koochiching Company turned to local capital. This time it was not disappointed. The year 1900 found it in contact with Brooks and Backus, and a reorganization of the company resulted immediately. Backus became president, Winchell first vice-president, Brooks second vice-president, and Rockwood secretary. Winchell had interested Rockwood; Rockwood in turn had interested his close friend, Edward W. Backus.

Backus had grown up in Red Wing, though he was a native of New York State. At the moment he was exactly forty years of age. Although he had had some training at the University of Minnesota, he had not completed his course there, but had left in 1882 to become a bookkeeper for Lee and McCulloch, a lumber company of Minneapolis. In 1883 he bought out McCulloch, and in 1885 he purchased Lee's interest. The company then became E. W. Backus and Company. In 1894 it became the E. W. Backus Lumber Company, which in turn became the Backus and Brooks Company in 1899, when William L. Brooks entered the organization.

From that time until his death some thirty years later, Backus was the developer of the Rainy River country. He became associated with many enterprises, being a venturesome personality of great imagination. His Koochiching Company outlived him and went out of existence only recently; other companies of which he was a part, and most of which he directed, were the International Lumber Company, which carried on all the logging and railroading for the Minnesota and Ontario Paper Company and owned the great lumber mill at International Falls from 1909 to 1937; the International Improvement Company; the Keewatin Lumber Company, Limited; the Columbia Gold Mining Company; the Rainy River Lumber Company; the National Pole and Treating Company; and, most important of all, the Minnesota and Ontario Paper Company, with all its associate and subsidiary companies. It was this last company which, as soon as the dam was completed, began the making of paper and pulp, the major industry of the region from that day to the present. Its subsidiary companies have had charge of associated activities, such as logging and sawing timber on a grand scale, building the dam, erecting the bridge between Fort Frances and International Falls (the name given to Koochiching in 1904), constructing logging and common-carrier railroads in the area, and so forth. In all this whirlwind of activity Fort Frances and Kenora have participated almost as much as International Falls.

Even the reorganized Koochiching Company could not get the dam under way for four years after Backus became president, despite every effort. Riparian rights had to be acquired on the Canadian shore at the falls; and, since the river was a boundary water, approval of the proposed construction had to be obtained from both the government of Canada and the War Department of the United States. Finally, in 1905, all the major difficulties had been overcome and work on the dam began. Only the residents of the locality and others privileged to see the great structure take form can have any adequate idea of the herculean task that faced the company, the engineers, and others who performed the feat of harnessing Rainy Lake's vast reservoir of water and drawing it up to the doors of International Falls and Fort Frances. When the work ended in 1910, the falls that had given their name to a region, a county, a town, a hotel, and many local geographical features were a thing of the past. Great turbines in mammoth hydroelectric powerhouses, on both sides of the river where the falls used to be, now seize the rushing torrent and convert it into electric power for pulp and other mills, for illumination of cities, and for other services.

To get pulp and paper one must first have timber. The feed for the grinders at International Falls came mostly from the area immediately south. Yet pine forests were spotty in northern Minnesota. Vast stands of white and Norway pine on the Mesabi hills delighted the souls of all who beheld them. To the north of that range were smaller and more scattered units, extending approximately to ten miles north of Virginia. Then, as one traveled northward, came thinly scattered timber of little commercial value, until one reached the site of Orr. Thence northward grew reasonably good blocks of timber worth cutting — fifty-five per cent, roughly, of the entire stand. Of this fifty-five per cent, twenty was Norway and thirty-five white pine. Although the pine was not so large nor so free from defects as the stands of Michigan and more southerly Minnesota, in this northern area from Vermilion Lake to Red Lake grew also a dense covering of lesser trees that were valuable for paper mills: spruce pre-eminently, balsam, aspen or popple, and tamarack. There was also much white cedar.

Most of the pine was harvested between 1910 and 1928.

FORT FRANCES IN THE EARLY 1900's
[Courtesy Minnesota and Ontario Paper Company.]

The Alexander Baker Homestead

[From a photograph owned by Paul Anderson.]

ALEXANDER BAKER
[From a photograph owned by Paul Anderson.]

MINNESOTA AND ONTARIO PAPER COMPANY PLANT, INTERNATIONAL FALLS, ABOUT 1912

[Courtesy Minnesota and Ontario Paper Company.]

B. D. and A. D.

During that time two Bunyanesque organizations felled the monarchs of this forest land with a speed and businesslike efficiency that were amazing. One was a subsidiary of the Minnesota and Ontario Paper Company, the International Lumber Company, which operated west of the eastern border of Koochiching County; the other was the Virginia and Rainy Lake Lumber Company, which operated east of Koochiching County as far as a line drawn south from Lac La Croix. Whereas the Virginia and Rainy Lake company withdrew as soon as the pine was cut on its rectangle of land, stretching south for fifty miles, the other company remained in operation until 1937; and logging has been continued for the Minnesota and Ontario Paper Company even after this subsidiary ended its career.

In 1907 the Weyerhaeuser interests at Cloquet — the Northern Lumber Company and the Cloquet Lumber Company, which jointly owned the Mesabi and Southern Railway and the Duluth and Northeastern Railway — sent Frank A. Gillmor to investigate the timber resources of the rectangle of land that they afterwards logged. On his cruising trip, which lasted exactly a year, Gillmor met Backus and his men, exploring for the same purpose. Both Gillmor and Backus were evidently satisfied with what they found, for two companies came into being very shortly for the purpose of cutting the timber that had been examined. Backus' company was the International Lumber Company, which was established in 1909 and remained in existence until 1937; Gillmor's sponsors became the Virginia and Rainy Lake Lumber Company, which, organized in 1908, operated for twenty years. The latter owned and operated at Virginia the largest white pine sawmill in the world. Gillmor's chiefs were some of the outstanding lumbermen of the country: the Weyerhaeusers, Edward Hines of Chicago, William O'Brien of Marine, Minnesota, and Wirt Cook of Duluth. The last two had organized the Minnesota Land and Construction Company and were logging in the vicinity of Virginia, where they had built a logging railroad out to their operations near Sand Lake. The Cloquet company had been logging around Mountain Iron and Virginia and east on the Mesabi Range almost to Biwabik. Gillmor had been in charge of its Mesabi and Southern railroads and logging operations since 1901. Now he was put in charge of the railroads and logging operations of the new company formed by these four giants of the logging business and some others. Hines persuaded the Canadian Northern to supply steel for building a railroad to connect Cook and O'Brien's logging road near Virginia with the border at Fort Frances, in return for the privilege of hauling all the new company's logs to Virginia. The railroad has had several names; it was first called the Duluth, Rainy Lake, and Winnipeg; today it is the Duluth, Winnipeg, and Pacific, a part of the Canadian National Railways. It does not touch International Falls, but crosses Rainy River to Fort Frances at Ranier.

The Virginia and Rainy Lake Lumber Company became the largest logging and milling company in Minnesota. In its first season, 1909–10, the log cut scaled 114,720,770 board feet; some twenty-eight hundred men were employed annually from September 1 to April 30, and about seventeen hundred from May 1 to September. This did not include the twelve hundred mill hands in Virginia, where there were two sawmills operating twenty-four hours a day; nor did it include the employees at the mill in Duluth.

Logging and railroad headquarters were at Cusson, a new village founded by the company on the Duluth, Winnipeg, and Pacific fifty miles north of Virginia. It was named for a cruiser, S. J. Cusson, just as its near neighbor, Gheen, was named for another, Stephen Gheen. It is said that Cusson was built at a cost of $83,000 dollars. There, among other structures, were headquarters buildings, a coal dock, icehouses, a boiler house, a warehouse, a hay shed, a timber shed, a pump house, a doctor's office, residences, a general store, a schoolhouse, a theater, rooming houses, a recreation building, and a machine shop where locomotives were repaired, cars were made and repaired, and similar work was performed.

In its twenty years of operation this company built approximately two thousand miles of branch railroads, or about a hundred miles a year. Two steel gangs did nothing but pick up and re-lay tracks as logging was completed in one area and begun in another. In addition, about a hundred miles of sleigh roads were graded every year, over which logs were hauled to the nearest rail branch or main line. There were fourteen standard locomotives, ten steam log haulers, and numerous gasoline boats, besides three loading cars, fifteen handcars, a sliding log loader, a Bucyrus steam shovel, three hundred and forty-five flatcars, snow and gravel plows, a pile driver, other cars, and cabooses.

Over these roads and railroads passed logs that became approximately 2,500,000,000 feet of manufactured lumber, which cost about $30,500,000 in logging and railroad operations alone. In addition to the other equipment, there were hoists for taking logs out of lakes and streams and placing them on cars for shipment to the Virginia sawmills. Some of the hoists were located on the following lakes, to which the logs were brought in many instances by driving streams: Rainy, Namakan, Kabetogama, Elbow, Black Duck, Johnson, Beaudoin, Ash, Elephant, and Echo. Serving the hoists were two "alligators," or amphibious tugs, which not only operated in water but could be seen waddling overland between lakes, like some ponderous antediluvian reptiles. On an average, there were fifteen logging camps at any moment, scattered through the north country, each with about a hundred and fifty men and eighteen teams of horses, all costing the company close to $150,000 annually for food, and producing enough logs to load daily more than twenty-five cars per camp.

The International Lumber Company had almost two hundred camps in the first thirty years or so of the Minnesota and Ontario Paper Company's logging. In 1917, the peak year of logging, there were twenty-three camps. In them more than four thousand men were employed annually, as well as about five hundred horses. Most of the horses were rented from farmers of the Red River Valley or from road contractors. In summer the horses helped to make roads in southern Minnesota; in winter they were taken up to haul logs in the north woods. By 1940 tractors of the caterpillar type had largely replaced horses in woods work. The sawmill of this company employed about four hundred men each season. It sawed mostly pine, but also a smaller amount of oak, elm, birch, and spruce. A lonely reminder of its former significance for the area is its tall burner, still standing silhouetted against the evening sky along the International Falls river front above the paper mills.

In 1916 Robert Fritz took charge of the mill at International Falls and remained there until its close in 1937. Prior to 1916 Mr. Fritz was in charge of the Swallow and Hopkins mill at Winton, another focus of sawmill activity on the fringes of the Rainy Lake country. At Winton also was the mill of the St. Croix Lumber Company, purchased by Edward Hines in 1911, when its name became the St. Croix Lumber and Manufacturing Company. It was famous for its log drives in the country just east of Vermilion Lake, for its entire transportation was performed by drives until about 1913. Then steam haulers began to supplant the earlier haulage methods of the company, as they had commenced ten years or so earlier to be important substitutes for railroads for some other north woods companies. These original ancestors of the bulldozers of today seem to have been born in northern Minnesota pineries, where they employed steam engines, mounted above caterpillar traction, to pull cars of logs to railroad sidings. In front of the tractor part of the contraption were sled runners. Here was the creation by the logging industry of a basic piece of mechanized equipment which was to be utilized throughout the world in the form of crawler type equipment. The efficient, caterpillar-driven bulldozer, used so extensively in World War II, thus had its beginning in Minnesota woodlands.

Mr. Gillmor and Mr. Fritz, as well as some others who witnessed the logging of northern Minnesota in the years after 1910, have drawn for the author a composite sketch of a winter in a typical logging camp. The older practices of New England, Michigan, and southern Minnesota camps lingered on, but they were gradually replaced by more modern ways. Log camps were often replaced by board and tar-paper structures; railroads were substituted for river drives; steam haulers and, later, tractors took the place of the horse, the bobsled, and the go-devil; double-decker iron beds replaced the aisles of wooden bunks that, it is said, gave the Pullman Company its idea of sleeping-car equipment; and Scandinavians, French-Canadians, Finns, Indians, and "Austrians" (Slovenians) filled the roles formerly acted by "Down-Easters" and "Blue Noses."

Rainy River Country

All the narrators' eyes sparkled at the remembrance of logging-camp food. "The best ever," was their unanimous verdict, as they recited the menus. In every camp of from a hundred to a hundred and fifty men there were usually a chief cook, two or more assistant cooks, and several cookees, besides a bull cook, a watchman, and sometimes others. Pies and other pastry, cakes, bread, and doughnuts were all made in the camp. Sour dough was more than a picturesque phrase in those logging days. Beans were baked chiefly in ovens, but the great three-legged iron pot for bean-hole cooking still lingered here and there. Mr. Fritz's favorite dish was "larrigan" pie, similar to lemon pie but made with vinegar. All the food was served on long tables, where the Wedgwood service was tin plates and cups, and where metal knives, forks, and spoons were the sterling flatware. Instead of sparkling dinner conversation complete silence was enforced in the interest of speed and peace. Fresh beef, pork, and sausage were the regular meats, but moose meat and venison — sometimes even a bear steak — were frequently added from the local stockyards, that is, the forests.

A typical logging camp consisted of three bunkhouses, a cook camp, a combined commissary and office, a barn, a blacksmith shop, a saw-filer's shack, a root house, sometimes a coal dock, and a few other structures. Buildings were constructed chiefly of Norway pine or unfinished lumber. There is a superstition among lumberjacks that usually prevents building a camp of aspen or "popple" logs.

The life of a Virginia and Rainy Lake logging camp averaged two and a half years. Then it was taken down and the windows, doors, and frames were moved to another location in the woods, and the rest was burned, as a rule. Approximately a million feet of logs were cut each working day between September 1 and April 30, the period when the lumberjacks could fell trees. There were usually in reserve in lakes and rivers between thirty-five and forty million feet to occupy the men at hoists and on the drives during the summer months.

Both companies' camps set the traditional bountiful tables of north woods lumber camps. In 1936 the average daily bread and pastry consumption of a Minnesota and Ontario Paper Company camp was forty-eight loaves of bread and forty pies. Detailed lists of food for Virginia and Rainy Lake company camps for 1919 show 686,855 pounds of fresh beef, 25,660 pounds of fresh veal, 28,255 pounds of bologna, 33,098 pounds of frankfurters, 52,979 pounds of ham, and 94,704 pounds of salt pork, besides other meat like liver, bacon, and pork sausage. The total "meat products" bill amounted to $172,061.56. For vegetables, including potatoes, onions, cabbage, rutabagas, beets, carrots, and some others, the account was $10,330.49. Wheat flour, 356,911 pounds, cost $18,647.52; and the rest of the total flour bill of $22,721.20 was paid for barley, rye, and some other flours.

When a lumberjack arrived in camp, his first job in the early part of this era was to get his bunk ready for the night. Usually this meant cutting balsam boughs or marsh hay for a mattress. Bunks were in double tiers on the long sides of the bunkhouse, down the center of which ran an aisle occupied in part with the big-bellied, or barrel, stove. Above the stove were lines on which to dry damp socks and mittens after a day of winter snow in the woods — and to supply the evening hours with an indescribable aroma. Blankets were usually furnished by the company, but pillows were concocted by the ingenuity of the lumberjack, frequently from his turkey sack stuffed with his few extra clothes.

Rainy River Country

Sunday was washday. Then a fire was built under the great iron kettle of water outdoors, and woolen socks, long underwear, bright shirts, and bandana handkerchiefs sent up great clouds of steam from the stumps on which the jacks placed their wash buckets. On other days, "Daylight in the swamp!" in the stentorian tones of a cookee or bull cook roused the sleeping lumberjacks at dawn or even earlier. After the ample breakfast, differing little from supper, everyone departed to his work — teamster, top loader, sawyer, swamper, undercutter, skidder, scaler, road monkey, stamper, and all the rest. Lunch was served hot in the woods from the swingdingle, or sleigh buffet. Supper came at the end of a strenuous day in close touch with Nature: purple shadows on the snow; dark pines; spruce hens and whisky-jacks making temporary friendships with the other jacks at the cost of a bit of their lunches; red squirrels chattering; snowshoe rabbits fleeting by; a pink-eyed weasel occasionally vanishing into a hole like a white streak; the broad palms of a moose's antlers waving, their owner crashing away into the dark recesses of the woods; the white flag of a bounding deer. Work of this kind for six days, washing and a little rest on Sundays, ample food, physical weariness that demanded an early bedtime — all added up to a life with little room or desire for carousal. That came later.

Mr. Gillmor's evaluation of the lumberjack of these and other camps, in which he spent forty years, is high compared with the rating given in the lurid accounts of books and articles appearing in recent years and written by men whose experience with such camps is wholly vicarious. He says that by no means all the lumberjacks "blew their stakes" every spring. Some saved enough to live well, though frugally, in very respectable hotels during the summers. Many were self-

NOON LUNCH FROM THE SWINGDINGLE
[Courtesy Zweifel-Rolleff Studio, Duluth.]

STEAM HAULER, INTERNATIONAL FALLS
[Courtesy Minnesota and Ontario Paper Company.]

A MODERN LUMBER CAMP

[Courtesy Minnesota and Ontario Paper Company.]

respecting, well-educated, family men. They saved their earnings and supported wives and children as any American head of a family did and does. Some were men of real education, who had come to the woods for a specific reason. One was a lawyer who was curing himself of alcoholism. As no liquor was allowed in camps, this man was cured, and he became the attorney of a large firm in Chicago at a high salary.

Mr. Gillmor remembers well the religious services held in the Virginia and Rainy Lake camps by nuns, missionaries, and others. Especially bright in his memory are Francis Edmund (Frank) Higgins and his convert, John Sorenberger, an ex-lumberjack and ex-pugilist. Both were Presbyterian missionaries who devoted their time to lumber camps in northern Minnesota.

Books and articles have told the fascinating story of Frank Higgins, most famous of all the sky pilots in the Rainy River country. Born in Toronto on August 19, 1865, of Irish-Canadian stock, he had practically no early formal education, but later as an adult he went back to school with youngsters, then had about two years of work in the preparatory department of Hamline University in St. Paul, and preached for a time at the little Methodist Church at Annandale. In 1895 he was appointed to a small Presbyterian church at Barnum, a logging town of about four hundred persons. At that place, where the drives on Kettle River passed, Higgins became interested in lumberjacks and felt the call to devote his life to these neglected men in northern Minnesota. His parish became two hundred square miles of forest.

Standing five feet nine inches and weighing two hundred pounds, he was big, jovial, rotund, and rosy-cheeked. Over the trails he carried huge packs loaded with books, magazines, and other reading matter for his jacks. He preached in bunkhouses night after night, simply but effectively, using the men's own language. One author in 1909 wrote: "He preaches every day and twice and three times a day—in the bunk houses, and he buries his boys—and marries them to the kind of women they know—and scolds and beseeches and thrashes them, and banks for them." One French-Canadian jack, who refused to be co-operative during a service and insisted on filing a saw, was seized by the preacher, after repeated requests to desist, and ducked headfirst in the rain barrel. Then he was set on his feet again without comment and Higgins continued the service in great equanimity, showing no signs of agitation or resentment.

Deer River was the Mecca for these recreation-starved men, and so Deer River stood for Sodom and Gomorrah in Higgins' sermons. Listen to him preach on the Prodigal Son: "And what did the young man do? . . . why, he packed his turkey and went off to blow his stake—*just like you!* . . . What about him *then*, boys? *You* know. *I* don't have to tell you. You learned all about it at Deer River. . . . It's up the river for you—and its back to the woods for you—when they've cleaned you out at Deer River!"

Higgins was always at Deer River after the spring drive, ready to guide his jacks safely past temptation, holding their money for them while they caroused in saloons and dives, seeing them and their money safely back to camp or on the train for home. One man who had tried eight successive seasons to get through Deer River with his roll finally succeeded the ninth time with Higgins' help.

The sky pilot was a fine singer, and the jacks loved to sing. "An amazing incongruity, these seared, blasphemous barbarians bawling, 'What a Friend I have in Jesus!' . . . 'Pilot,' said one of them in open meeting once, with no irreverence whatsoever, 'that's a damned fine toon! Why the hell don't they have toons like that in shows? Let's sing her again!' 'Sure,' said the preacher, not at all shocked, 'let's sing her again!' "

The great packsacks finally chafed and irritated Higgins' neck and shoulders too much. He died at the outbreak of World War I of cancer of the collar bones.

Another missionary in the general area visited the Swallow and Hopkins camp near Basswood Lake every month. The cook of that camp now remembers him only as "Jerusalem Slim," the men's name for him. In fact, the men had their sobriquets for nearly everyone. The hobo lumberjack who stayed a day or two and then moved on was a "camp walker," or "walking daily," or perhaps "camp inspector." The walking boss was often called a "push." The camp for the odoriferous teamsters and other men associated with horses was sometimes called the "skinners' camp." "Hungry Joe," "Two Bit Shorty," "Pegleg Dave," the "Ace of Clubs" (barn boss), "Stony Slim" were some of the nicknames in one camp. The men there also called the 'gator the "rambler" or "slough hog." Men on the drives there, as everywhere in logging country, were "river pigs."

In fur-trading days the borderland had its chorusing voyageurs. Later it had its singing lumberjacks. Although the language changed and the meters were not so refined, the songs of the bunkhouses were as hearty and were enjoyed as much by the singers as the canoe songs had been. Mr. Gillmor recalls the singing of his men in Virginia and Rainy Lake camps — all the old Nova Scotia, Maine, and Michigan favorites among the comeallya's, from "Garry's Rock" to "The Maid of the Mountain Brow." With his kitchen chair tipped back and his eyes closed, no doubt remembering the scenes recalled by the air, Mr. Gillmor sang for the author in 1948 many of the almost interminable stanzas of that little-known song, which was a prime favorite forty years ago:

The Maid of the Mountain Brow *

Come all ye men and maidens and listen to my song,
And if you'll pay attention I'll not detain you long.
'Twas of a wealthy young man I'm going to tell you now,
And he's lately become a member of the Maid of the Mountain
    Brow.

He said, "My lovely fair maid, if you'll come along with me now
We'll go and we'll get married and it's happy we will be.
We'll join our hands in wedlock bands if you'll come along with
    me now.
I will labour late and early for the Maid of the Mountain Brow.

She being a wigglesome young thing she didn't know what to say.
Her eyes did sparkle like diamonds and as merrily she did play:
"Kind sir, I would rather be excused, I can't go with you now.
I will tarry another season at the foot of the Mountain Brow."

He said, "My lovely fair maid, how can you answer no?
Look down in yonder valley where my crops do gently grow.
Look down in yonder valley stands my horses and my plow.
They work both late and early for the Maid of the Mountain
    Brow."

"If they work both late and early, kind sir, it's not for me.
Your conduct it is none of the best, for I can plainly see.
There is an inn where you call in, for I've heard people say,
Where you rap and call and pay for all, and go home at the break
    of day."

"If I rap and call and pay for all, my money it is my own,
"If I rap and call and pay for all, my money it is my own,

* Reprinted from William R. Mackenzie, *Ballads and Sea Songs from Nova Scotia* (Cambridge, 1928), by permission of Harvard University Press.

You thought you had my poor heart gained by happening on
  me now,
But I'll leave you where I met you at the foot of the Mountain
  Brow."

"O it's Jimmy dear, it's Jimmy, how can you be so unkind!
To a girl you loved so dearly how quickly you've changed your
  mind,
To a girl you loved so dearly, and you're going to leave me now.
O don't leave me broken hearted at the foot of the Mountain
  Brow."

Two railroads reached Rainy River in 1907. The Northern
Pacific, induced by certain influential stockholders with
Koochiching Company affiliations, continued to International
Falls the logging railroad that had already been built from
Brainerd to Bemidji; it was called the Minnesota and International and is now a part of the Northern Pacific. Simultaneously the Virginia and Rainy Lake Lumber Company,
with aid from the Canadian Northern, extended its logging
railroad from just north of Virginia to Ranier and Fort
Frances, as already noted. These two roads were common
carriers as well as important parts of the logging operations
of both the Virginia and Rainy Lake Lumber Company and
the Minnesota and Ontario Paper Company, frequently called
by its abbreviated name, "Mando." There were a few other
common carriers in the region, but most of the spiderwork of
rails was temporary, and has vanished. One of the common
carriers was the Minnesota, Dakota, and Western, which was
organized in 1909 to serve the International Falls industry
and make connections with logging railroads. It was the tan-
gible part of a grandiose dream of Backus. Eighteen miles
of track were actually built west toward the Dakota wheat
fields, whose products were to be hauled to huge flour mills

in International Falls. As the mills never developed, the so-
called Loman line was used for hauling logs, especially from
the hoist at Loman on the river.

Besides the common-carrier lines, the International Lumber
Company built and operated at various times a total of
twenty-five hundred miles of logging railroads. At the peak
of operations in 1917 rolling stock included eleven locomotives, a hundred and fifty flatcars, work cars, cabooses, steam
shovels, and fire-fighting cars. The greatest number of miles
of road in any one season was approximately two hundred.

One of the principal logging roads of this company was
the Deer River branch, built in 1912–14 and dismantled in
1947. It extended from a point on the Minnesota and International below Littlefork to Craig (Craigville), where a headquarters camp has been maintained for many years. Spurs ran
out into northern parts of Itasca County and west central
parts of St. Louis County, as the Holmstrom spur; west from
Littlefork, as the Bear River line; and south from International
Falls, by way of seven miles on the Minnesota and International, as the Galvin branch. Backus had planned to join his
Deer River division at Craig with the old "Guts and Liver
Line," that is, the Minneapolis and Rainy River, which had
been extended northward from Deer River to the south bank
of the Big Fork at Craig. There the two lines halted and
looked longingly across the river at each other, but they were
never joined. The Minneapolis and Rainy River, a common
carrier, had been built by the Itasca Lumber Company of
Deer River, and it carried a heavy volume of timber from
1906 to 1923, its life span. Another vision that never material-
ized was the proposed extension of the Holmstrom spur to a
connection with the Soo line at Pengilly on the Mesabi Iron
Range.

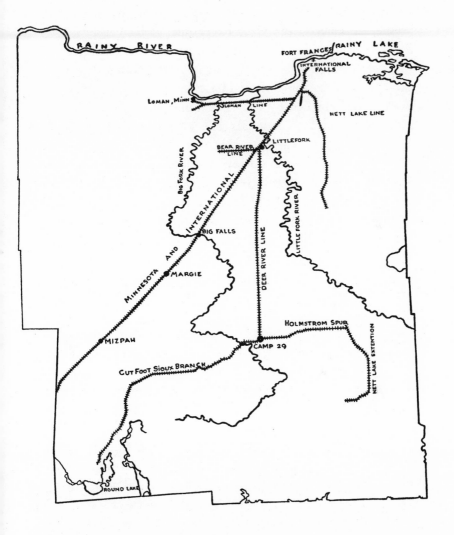

NORTHERN MINNESOTA LOGGING RAILROADS OF THE MINNESOTA AND
ONTARIO PAPER COMPANY, 1910–47

Rainy River Country

Besides Loman, the Mando logging company had other hoists: at Craig on the Deer River line; at Beaver Brook on the Galvin branch; at Round Lake on the Cutfoot Sioux; at Harrigan Lake, reached by a spur from the Nett Lake extension, itself an extension of the Holstrom spur; and on the Little Fork River, reached by the "Pea Vine Line," that is, by the Minnesota and International. The biggest railroad year for Mando operations was 1928, when 153 miles of main line and 70 of spur track were in operation. All told, between 1914 and 1947 the railroads of the company carried two million cords of wood, or five thousand flatcars, a year.

Woods and railroad operations were by no means the only activities of Mando, even in the early years of the company's existence. After the dam was completed, the paper mill was begun, and it was completed in 1910. That year a bridge was constructed across Rainy River to Fort Frances. In 1911 the huge sawmill was built at International Falls. In 1914 the Fort Frances Pulp and Paper Company, Limited, a subsidiary of Mando, finished its mill and commenced the manufacture of paper at Fort Frances. In 1923 the Kenora Paper Mills, Limited, another subsidiary, began to build a paper mill at Kenora. In 1927 the Seine River was developed electrically, and the Great Lakes Paper Company's plant was built at Fort William. All these and other enterprises were the brain children of the same company, which, as reorganized in 1941, with the exception of the Great Lakes Paper Company, is known in the United States as the Minnesota and Ontario Paper Company, and in Canada as the Ontario-Minnesota Pulp and Paper Company, Limited. The latter is an amalgamation of Kenora Paper Mills, Limited, the Keewatin Power Company, Limited, the Keewatin Lumber Company, Limited, the Fort Frances Pulp and Paper Company, Limited, and the Ontario and Minnesota Power Company, Limited.

FORT FRANCES FROM INTERNATIONAL FALLS RIVER FRONT, 1912
[Courtesy Minnesota and Ontario Paper Company.]

THIRD STREET, INTERNATIONAL FALLS, 1909
[Courtesy Minnesota and Ontario Paper Company.]

MAIN STREET, RAT PORTAGE (KENORA), 1881
[Courtesy Minnesota and Ontario Paper Company.]

BUILDING THE DAM

[Courtesy Minnesota and Ontario Paper Company.]

B. D. and A. D.

In 1907, while the dam was building and just after the destructive fire of 1905, which nearly wiped out the village, Fort Frances began the construction of modern civic improvements. First came sewers, then waterworks. In the following years, and until 1911, there was much trouble between the village and the local industrial company on the head of water power and taxes. Meantime, the sawmill history of the place was similar to that of the other Rainy River communities, such as Rainy River, Spooner, Baudette, and other places on both banks of the stream. There was the Preston-Bell sawmill on Rainy Lake; the Christie-Sissons mill, which became the Northern Construction Company of McKenzie and Mann, the builders of the Canadian Northern railway system; the mill of J. A. Mathieu, Limited; the twin mills of Shevlin-Clarke, Limited, at Rainy River, erected in 1913, two years after the Rainy River Lumber Company's plant there had been dismantled; and the Lockhart Lumber Company's mill on Rocky Inlet. The great Shevlin-Mathieu mill was established at Spooner in 1905. Its cut was over sixty million feet a year, and it employed about three hundred and fifty men working both day and night shifts. The mill burned in 1921.

The Norman dam, at the western outlet of Lake of the Woods, was built in 1892 by the Keewatin Power Company, Limited, as a storage dam for the control of the lake levels. In 1913 it was bought by the Backus-Brooks interests, but it was not used for power purposes until 1923, when the present power plant was installed. In 1920 the municipal power plant built by the town of Kenora in 1906 at the eastern outlet of Lake of the Woods was sold to the Keewatin Power Company, which by then had become one of the Backus-Brooks interests. The first sawmill, erected by John Mather, a veteran lumberman from the Ottawa Valley, began operations on the site of Keewatin as early as 1880. Its machinery had been brought from Minne-

apolis by way of the Red River to Winnipeg. Thence on
sleighs and wagons it was conveyed over the Dawson Trail
to the Northwest Angle, where barges took it and floated it
to Keewatin. The other mills in Rat Portage, Norman, and
Keewatin have been listed. One of the early lumbermen who
started logging operations centering in the Rat Portage area
was Donald McLeod, who later was vice-president of Backus
and Brooks and still later of the Ontario and Minnesota Pulp
and Paper Company. David Low Mather, son of John, was
another important lumberman of Lake of the Woods district.
It is said that he supplied twenty million railroad ties in his
long sawmill career. During the heyday of milling in Rat
Portage thousands of islands in the lake were pretty well de-
nuded of their conifers, so that the name of this magnificent
seventy-mile stretch of water, islands, and woods was no
longer appropriate. But time heals many scars, and today the
islands are largely wooded once more, though not with pines.

Today in the Borderlands

It is a far cry from the pines, caribou, and Indians of McLoughlin's day to the grasslands, farms, and industrialized cities of 1950 in the Rainy River country. Whereas the river was uppermost in men's minds in former times, the two lakes at its ends feature more largely today. Increasingly since 1890 tourists and sportsmen have been attracted to these immense bodies of water, especially since the advent of good roads in the 1920's and 1930's, and the consequent use of automobiles. Until the middle 1930's there was no road along the south shore of Rainy Lake, and even today Highway 11, a stretch of a dozen miles or so, is the only means of access from the American side. There is hardly more on the Canadian shore.

Highway 11 extends west from Black Bay of Rainy Lake through Ranier and International Falls to the Red River of the North, passing through most of the villages and hamlets that constitute the chief American communities of the Rainy River country: Pelland, Loman, Spooner, Baudette, Warroad, and Roseau. Littlefork, Big Falls, Ericsburg, Ray, Cusson, and Orr are on the two main highways, 53 and 71, leading south to Virginia and Bemidji, respectively. Across the river from Highway 11 runs the old River Road on the Canadian side, which is identified for some miles with the recently finished main highway, number 70, connecting Fort Frances and Kenora. This is a scenic thoroughfare running through forests, lakes, and granite crags. It strikes Lake of the Woods at Nestor Falls and follows the deeply indented shoreline more or less for the remainder of the way.

In 1948 a map was put out by Rand McNally and Company, entitled *Northern Great Lakes Area Conservation-Recreation Map*, featuring Minnesota and near-by states and Canadian provinces. The basic map is white; on it state, dominion, provincial, and national parks and forests, Indian reservations, game preserves, wild-life sanctuaries, and similar areas are colored. As one looks at the region north and west of Lake Superior, one cannot fail to be struck by the concentration of color in the Rainy River country. The great Superior National Forest forms a huge green block from Lake Superior to Crane Lake; north of it on the Canadian side lies Quetico Provincial Park, a big red patch dotted with an infinity of blue lakes; immediately west of it Kabetogama State Forest extends from Vermilion Lake almost to International Falls. The only white patch in this whole section, in fact, is about International Falls, Fort Frances, the American side of the river to Manitou Rapids, and the entire Canadian bank of the river. From Manitou Rapids to Muskeg Bay on Lake of the Woods is the huge Red Lake Game Preserve, which encloses Beltrami Island State Forest and touches Pine Island State Forest on the east. In turn, Pine Island State Forest touches Koochiching State Forest on the east, which in turn touches Nett Lake Indian Reservation, the final bit of colored frame enclosing the white center of International Falls and its neighborhood. There are also two big game preserves and several Indian reserves on the Canadian side between Fort Frances and Kenora. Thus the map indicates graphically why the tourist and the sportsman visit the Rainy River country every summer. Here Nature has been given a breathing space and still heals men's minds and spirits with the balm of her peace.

Lake of the Woods — 1,485 square miles of blue water and rocky islands — has been developed, tourist-wise, more than Rainy Lake, which is just beginning to exhibit summer homes and tourist resorts beyond Ranier; but neither lake has reached the saturation point, and both are definitely "wild" still. Both have almost countless islands—Lake of the Woods boasts fourteen thousand, Rainy Lake some thousands fewer. Seventy per cent of the waters of Lake of the Woods and most of the islands are Canadian. The lake derives its water from a drainage basin which is forty-two per cent in the United States and the remainder in Canada. But the United States owns the famous Northwest Angle, a hundred and thirty square miles of American soil attached to Canada, jutting into Lake of the Woods, and nowhere connected with the rest of the state or country to which it belongs. It has the distinction of being the northernmost point of the forty-eight states. It is a state forest, where efforts are being made to honor more properly the remains of old Fort St. Charles among the trees. Indians called the southern part of the lake "Lake of the Sand Hills," whereas the northern part was termed "Lake of Islands," emphasizing the striking difference between the American and Canadian portions. Oddly enough, the boundary commissioners of 1823 ran the line almost precisely along the natural, geological line, where glacial drift ended as the ice sheets receded.

For twenty-five years or so the *Field and Stream* contests for big fish have been won by Lake of the Woods products, including muskies, lake trout, small-mouth bass, wall-eyed pike, and great northern pike. Besides these varieties, crappies, rock bass, whitefish, bullheads, perch, and sturgeon abound. Salmon or lake-trout fishing in eastern Lake of the Woods is outstanding. Sabaskong Bay has been popular with fishermen for many years. In autumn duck and geese hunters also flock to the lake and its environs, where wild rice feeding grounds attract thousands of migratory wild fowl.

Since Brown's day, as recorded minutely in his diaries for

the years from 1889 to 1901, the south shore of Lake of the Woods has been famous for deer hunting. In his time there was also excellent hunting for moose, caribou, and elk. Reading these diaries gives one the thrill of following all those great, wary animals through muskeg and snow-covered brush country, sometimes to the kill, often merely for the exercise entailed, along with the exhilaration of seeing Nature completely unposed, in stern but lofty mood. With the advance of settlers, the burning of forest mold, and the drainage of swamps, these animals receded to Canada. In such public areas as the wild-life sanctuaries and game preserves, however, one may still see the only elk herd of Minnesota, some three hundred animals; a rare caribou; and a concentration of moose. In Lake of the Woods County, created in 1922, as elsewhere in the Rainy River country, one may still see ruffed, pinnated, spruce, and sharp-tailed grouse, timber and brush wolves, bear, lynx, snowshoe hares, mink, otter, marten, many beaver, and a few other rarer animals. In Brown's day it was one of the chief American regions for nesting wild fowl, but drainage of swamps and the encroachment of settlers have diminished greatly the number of these and other birds, including the swans, sandhill cranes, whooping cranes, Eskimo and other curlews, plovers, pelicans, geese, godwits, many kinds of wading birds, many warblers, the American hawk owl, Richardson's owl, the great gray owl, many woodpeckers, the northern raven, the Hudsonian as well as the black-capped chickadee, crossbills, and evening and pine grosbeaks. Only in this part of their country may Canadians see cormorants and turkey vultures. Great fires helped to destroy the region's teeming wild creatures. The fur traders told of the terrible fires of their days, including those of 1734 and 1803–04. Winchell in 1887 found evidences of a much more recent conflagration.

Another fearful fire raged in 1894. In 1910 Baudette and Spooner were wiped out and had to rebuild. There were many other fires.

A feature of wild life in Lake of the Woods that is utilized for local industry is the rough fish, the freshwater variety of the codfish, known variously as the burbot, eelpout, or lawyer *(Lota maculosa)*. In Baudette a burbot-liver-products company has been established for some years, and it makes use of the liver of this fish for the extraction of an oil with a high vitamin A content, and with a vitamin D potency some eight times greater than that of cod-liver oil. At the industrial plant, which employs about thirty persons, the oil is put up in bottle, capsule, and ointment form.

Like other parts of northern Minnesota, the Rainy River basin waited for the pine lumbermen to finish their tasks before many permanent settlers arrived and modern agricultural and industrial development began. Around Lake of the Woods forests were never of such importance as elsewhere in the basin, and so settlement began there somewhat earlier than in the valleys of the Vermilion, Rapid, Little Fork, Rat Root, and Big Fork rivers; for the great green forest extended west only to Warroad.

Although it belongs to the Red River basin, Roseau and some of its neighbor communities seem tied to the economy of the Rainy River country. Here one finds the best sheep country of Minnesota. Another sheep-raising region of some fame is the stretch between Loman and Baudette on Rainy River. Roseau itself is a thriving industrial village as well as a dairy and agricultural center. It has a milk-drying plant for a large co-operative, which depends for its milk on creameries as far east as Spooner and as far west as Greenbush. There is also a co-operative creamery at Roseau, which produces over half a million pounds of butter annually. Co-operatives, in fact, are an integral part of the life of the Rainy River basin. Salol has a co-operative elevator, erected in 1941, which handles about 200,000 bushels of grain. Warroad has a co-operative creamery, which produces approximately 550,000 pounds of butter annually. Other co-operative creameries are to be found at Greenbush, Badger, Loman, Northome, Spooner, and possibly other places.

The region between International Falls and the Red River of the North, as well as the area in Manitoba west of the Northwest Angle, is famous in agricultural circles for its legumes and its seed crops. Alfalfa, alsike, and other clover, potatoes, and grasses are grown for seed; and legume crops are also important sources of revenue. Potatoes are likewise raised for sale. Great yields of small grain and hay are common. Raspberries and blueberries are natural crops, well utilized by residents and Indians. More and more flax is being grown. Another new and successful business is bee culture, especially in the Manitoba area.

Part of the success of these rather specialized crops is the unusual soil combination. In many places it is clay loam on clay subsoil, the effect of glaciation and the presence of Glacial Lake Agassiz for so many years. In other places muskegs and peat swamps have been burned, after drainage by a costly process in some instances, leaving nitrogenous ashes on the soil. This process of soil making is especially evident about Salol, which originally was a clay island in the midst of a great peat swamp. During the 1930's the peat beds burned for months and even years, uncovering a soil which, when peat is added, makes sixteen thousand acres of unexcelled earth for raising legume, seed, and cereal crops.

As for industries in Koochiching, Lake of the Woods, and

MODERN MECHANIZED LOGGING

[Courtesy Minnesota and Ontario Paper Company.]

TWINE HOUSE AT OAK POINT, LAKE OF THE WOODS, 1901
[From a photograph owned by John Dobie.]

Roseau counties and neighboring parts of Canada, the main centers, of course, are Fort Frances, International Falls, and Kenora, but some of the smaller communities have their plants of various types, too. Ranier has some boat-building industry, besides being the center of the tourist trade of Rainy Lake; and, most significant, it is one of the most important American ports of entry on the border, collecting some half a million dollars or more in duties annually. Roseau produces electrodes for cast and malleable welding. Spooner has a cold-storage locker system of four hundred units, owned by the co-operative creamery. Warroad is the chief American port on Lake of the Woods, from which run mail and passenger steamers to the Northwest Angle, Kenora, and other lake localities. It is likewise the center of Minnesota's pen-raised mink business. Twenty per cent of the state's pen-raised mink are reared on ranches along the south shore of Lake of the Woods, where cold weather and a fine, cheap fish diet produce better than average pelts. In addition, there are expert fleshers at hand to remove the pelts from the flesh, for no one can approach an Indian woman in this business.

When the three main industrial centers are considered, their modern story is a unit in one sense, for all three depend for life and well-being on the same great industrial concern, the Minnesota and Ontario Paper Company. When the dam was completed in 1910, after Congressional interference had stopped work in 1907 for a year, it provided a thirty-foot head of water, whereas the original waterfall was only twenty-four feet in drop. The water comes from a drainage basin of 14,500 square miles of lakes, rocks, and forests, reaching down to Chisholm, Virginia, and other Mesabi Range towns, over to North Lake just beyond Gunflint Lake on the border, and far up into Ontario. Later, dams and powerhouses also were

Rainy River Country

erected at Moose Lake, Calm Lake, and Sturgeon Falls, all
in the Seine River system, which empties into the eastern end
of Rainy Lake. These power plants went into operation in
1927. There are also control dams at Kettle Falls, where
Namakan Lake pours into Rainy Lake. These were built
in 1914. The development of the Steep Rock iron mine during
the last war caused the discontinuance in 1943 of the Moose
Lake production. Its power is replaced by transmission from
the Thunder Bay system on Lake Superior. Since a hundred
miles of wire are required between Seine River developments
and International Falls, over wild and difficult terrain, some
of the engineering and other problems may be imagined. For
instance, at Rainy Lake crossing, about two miles of especially
difficult wiring cost thirty thousand dollars a mile.

Hydrological engineers are required by the industry. Their
records of rainfall and other data constitute a valuable body
of information on the amount of water that passes out of
the basin, how much is retained, how long a time is required
for moisture to pass from its source to the big dam at the falls,
and so forth. Generally speaking, twenty-eight per cent of
all water or snow which falls on the watersheds reaches the
dam, where the low-water point of the year is early April,
and the high point is just two months later. Rainy Lake, 345
square miles in area, acts as a great reservoir. Its power production is about sixty thousand horsepower. The Seine River
units add twenty-five thousand more by high voltage transmission wires; the Kenora powerhouse on Winnipeg River
and Norman dam supply twenty-three thousand horsepower.
International Falls and Fort Frances are lighted from the local
dam, and Kenora is supplied three thousand horsepower from
the Mando plant.

There were plans for many other dams in the original

scheme: at Lac La Croix and at Sturgeon, Birch, Garden, Basswood, Crooked, and Iron lakes. But citizens of both Canada and the United States were opposed to the raising of water levels far back along the border country toward Lake Superior, which would have spoiled both natural resources and scenery. The Quetico-Superior Council and other citizen organizations were formed and crusaded against the program, and they secured national legislation. In 1930 the Shipstead-Nolan Act was passed by Congress and signed by the president. It has blocked further erection of dams.

During the first thirty years of operation by the Mando pulp and paper mills, giant grinders and chippers gnawed away approximately six million cords of pulpwood, or the average yield of six hundred thousand acres of forest land. In addition, the sawmill cut slightly more than a billion board feet of lumber in its twenty-seven years of operation, or the average yield of about half a million acres. Thus from 1,100,000 acres, the sum of the two acreages, came merchantable timber and saw logs which were further processed into lumber, insulation board, and a wide variety of other pulp and paper products needed to satisfy the needs of millions. Since 1936, the natural reforestation of the area from which Mando gets its forest products has been aided by a tree-planting program. In one five-week period in 1948 more than half a million seedlings were planted, and during a similar period in 1949 over seven hundred thousand seedlings were set out.

The products of all this activity are varied and interesting, involving much chemical and other research. An entire building is devoted to research by a staff of highly trained persons. While newsprint was the original aim of the company, insulation material is now one of the chief products. Today the pulpwood is brought in partly by drives down Canadian rivers, partly by truck, partly by railroad. At the end of July, 1948, seventy-one thousand cords of spruce and jack pine were being driven down Little Turtle River, some hundred and forty miles, through seven dams or sluiceways, to Rainy Lake to be boomed and towed the rest of the way by tugboat.

In 1948 the International Falls plant employed nineteen hundred persons; the Kenora establishment had six hundred and fifty employees; and the Fort Frances mills gave work to eight hundred persons. A total of some five thousand woodsmen and others depend on the company for employment. The total company payroll was over sixteen and a half million dollars in 1948. The mills are giant kitchens and laundries, in which the contents of mammoth mixing bowls, stewing vats, and tubs are ground or chipped wood. After the proper washing and cooking by live steam — twenty million pounds are used daily by all the company's plants — the tons of pulp jell and, baked, become insulating board, or, ironed between great mangles, emerge as paper. A hundred and sixty miles of piping are required to convey the steam needed in the International Falls plant. Over 250 tons of various grades of paper go out of that mill every day; and over 1,250,000 square feet of insulating materials are wrapped and loaded into boxcars every day there. The Kenora plant makes newsprint, for which it has two paper machines out of the company's total of nine; produces 100,000 tons of paper annually; uses 117,000 cords of wood annually; and has an annual payroll of $3,500,000.

Both International Falls and Fort Frances have developed into modern cities since 1905, when the dam was begun. Back and forth over the bridge go the residents of the twin communities, just as though no international border lay between. Yet there are evidences of a dividing line, too, since border patrol officers — immigration and customs — are met on the bridge, where they inspect luggage and cars and question the owners. But even so, there is little to suggest that different flags float over the two river towns. Perhaps the fringes of International Falls are a little rough and new, as befits such a recently founded place; perhaps one can detect a cockney accent once in a while in Fort Frances. Both communities, however, pride themselves on excellent municipal improvements, fine schools, churches, paved streets, movie houses, tourist camps, broadcasting stations, newspapers, an airport, a community center, and so forth.

Many nationalities make up the population, but Finns, Slovenes, Poles, Ukrainians, and Scandinavians are especially numerous. From the Scots in the region undoubtedly arises the deep interest in curling, with bonspiels, particularly in Kenora. A winter carnival occurs annually in that place, where skiing, skating, curling, and other winter sports are much in evidence in the gaily bedecked community. International Falls has its Forest Festival in the autumn, with Paul Bunyan a prominent actor.

Besides being the industrial centers of the area, these three cities are still the focuses of vast logging operations. Some of the pulpwood is cut in the local company's own camps; the rest, forty-three per cent, is purchased, mostly from small, independent farmers, who may cut anywhere from ten to a hundred cords a season and send it to one of the three cities by truck. Some is transported by rail, and a small proportion still arrives by water. In the Kenora area about twenty-five per cent comes in by truck; at Fort Frances and International Falls, delivery is about evenly divided between truck and rail shipments. About seventeen hundred separate and independent producers engage in supplying logs cut in Minnesota. Canadian purchases for the three mills are placed at about 180,000 cords annually; about 170,000 cords are bought from Minnesota producers. Ninety per cent of the spruce and balsam purchased is delivered during the winter months, whereas jack pine and poplar are delivered throughout the year. The area in which these 350,000 cords of pulpwood are cut extends from Fort Frances west to Lake of the Woods and north to and including the Kenora district, besides the Fir River district in Saskatchewan; in Minnesota it extends over most of the northern part of the state. Small operators are aided by the company in locating and financing their stumpage, for they are farmers first and foremost, and they often lack the means for getting started in logging.

Fort Frances and Kenora are important logging-camp centers. In Ontario the company has cutting rights on four timber areas known as the Patricia, Lake of the Woods, Manitou, and Seine River concessions. These comprise an area of 5,021 square miles, or slightly more than 3,000,000 acres. The first two concessions supply wood to the Kenora mill and the others, to the Fort Frances mill. There are 18,000,000 cords of jack pine and spruce pulpwood on the four concessions; the two mills require 250,000 cords of pulpwood annually. In Minnesota the operating area from which the company obtains most of its mill requirements for the International Falls mills comprises about 4,000,000 acres. It owns about 200,000 acres of its own timberlands. One of the spots always visited by tourists in International Falls is the huge storage yard, to which approximately 275 trucks in the 1947–48 season hauled a total of 195,000 cords of logs. The operations mean a payroll of approximately $325,000 a month for woodsmen, camp employees, truckers, and others.

In line with the company's multimillion-dollar improvement program in operation since 1945, mechanization of logging operations in its own camps, and modernization of camp life make the average Ontario or Minnesota logging camp utterly different from anything ever known before. Realizing that old methods were wasteful and unappealing to the right sort of woodsmen, the company is abandoning old-style methods at a great rate. The logger of today tends to be young, married, and reasonably well educated and traveled. Hence he wants his family with him in surroundings that are appealing to women and children. The company puts up individual dwelling houses, as well as dormitories far out in the wilderness, where the camp is located. In the Patricia area, for example, where year-around operations are carried on, the camps are thirty miles from the nearest community. They are equipped with electric generating plants to supply power for lighting, power tools, refrigerators, other kitchen equipment, radio, water-pumping systems, and so forth. A hospital and a school are provided. There are even weekly movies, not to mention two-way radio systems that keep the community in touch with headquarters, where a plane, equipped for emergency landing on water, earth, or snow, is in readiness for take-off. Even log cutting in the woods and truck and car loading are now in process of mechanization.

With such a stake in the region and in the health and happiness of its inhabitants, there is no cause for wonderment that the company enters heartily into programs of civic improvement, school and hospital building, scholarships for deserving young people, elimination of river pollution, and other methods of making life easier, happier, and more satisfying to the people of the Rainy River country. Its own program of tree planting has been in force some years now, and it bids fair to help make Minnesota's acres yield in the not-too-distant future as much per unit as Sweden's, for example. There, where climatic conditions are much the same as in Minnesota, the average growth of all the forests is about one-third of a cord of pulpwood per acre a year, or more than three times the average annual growth in our unmanaged forests.

Tourists are an important part of borderland economy nowadays, and the region is geared to the needs and expectations of vacationists, fishermen, and hunters. Already there are many resorts on the little stretch of Rainy Lake's south shore accessible by road; and many islands in certain parts of the lake are utilized for summer homes and camps. Fishing is excellent in this lake, as well as in Lake of the Woods. Early every morning in summer the dawn stillness is interrupted by the put-put of many outboard motors carrying fishermen to their favorite grounds. At night they return to cottages or resorts, where Finnish *saunas*, or steam baths, are an attraction in many instances. Swimming from sand beaches is another attraction — not often to be offered by lakes so far north as Rainy Lake. A number of power launches and houseboats are to be seen on this great sheet of water, not to mention the tugs hauling immense booms of logs.

These big islands of logs, floating lazily near Fort Frances and Kenora, are symbols of the area. Men with pike poles move the logs along and feed them on to the end of a continuous moving conveyor called a "jack ladder." Thus they are taken into the wood room or storage yard, ready for grinding or chipping after being cut to the proper length and deprived of their bark.

Some other symbols of the region have been the birchbark canoe, the old river steamboats, the York boats, and wannigans. The first three have passed forever, but the last remains

AERIAL VIEW OF RAINY LAKE. LOG BOOMS IN FOREGROUND

[Courtesy Minnesota and Ontario Paper Company.]

ARNESEN FISHERY, LAKE OF THE WOODS
[Courtesy Minnesota Department of Conservation.]

LOADING FISH AT WARROAD
[Courtesy Minnesota Department of Conservation.]

A York Boat

[From *The Beaver*, March, 1949.]

THE OLD FISHERY ON ROCKY POINT, LAKE OF THE WOODS

[Photographed by John Dobie.]

under another name. Lest some reader has never witnessed a York boat on Arctic waters, or read of the unusual craft in explorers' and fur traders' accounts, it may be well to describe it before discussing the sole survivor of these four, formerly common sights on Rainy Lake, Rainy River, and Lake of the Woods. Probably these waters were the southernmost ever to float the York boat, for it was used primarily in the far Northwest. It was about twenty-eight feet long and strong enough to carry heavy sail and stand rough weather. It was worked with sweeps handled by a crew of six men and a steersman. In his reminiscences of Fort Frances, Biddison tells of the excitement occasioned there by the departure of brigades of York boats.

The wannigan was the supply and commissary boat attached to drives of logs. In the colorful pageant of the last great drive in this area — the 1937 drive of Nett Lake logs down Nett and Little Fork rivers to Rainy River — not the least important unit was the wannigan, trailing the rest of the show. One still hears of the "Wangan" or "Wangan Boats" on Lake of the Woods.

Thus transportation methods still tie the present to the past in the Rainy River country. The canoeist on Rainy Lake or Lake of the Woods still feels a genuine bond with David Thompson, Alexander Mackenzie, Dr. John McLoughlin, and John McKay. Even the common sight of Indians in powered canoes does not seem too incongruous in this setting of woods and waters. At least the canoes are still there — and the Indians are still present, despite all that has happened in the past two hundred years. It must be admitted that on three occasions — in 1812, when Tecumseh sent his couriers to Rainy River, in 1891, and again in 1900 — the natives seriously considered ejection of the whites by forcible

Rainy River Country

means from this fair land, but better counsel prevailed. A local bard has composed a long, narrative poem, telling how the well-known Vermilion Lake Indian, Wake 'Em Up, discouraged his neighboring tribesmen from joining the second Riel Rebellion. After describing the couriers sent out by Riel, this farmer-poet, in rude but convincing measures, lists the headmen who turned up at the council place near Manitou Rapids:

Where Little Fork has found a rest
In Rainy's wide and tranquil breast,
    The Council meet
    With hurrying feet
Chiefs from the East, and South, and West.

They came from far off Battle Lake
Through muskeg flat, and tangled brake.
    Red Sky is there
    With matted hair,
And Bombi-Gezek and Kee-Jee-Go-Kay.

Blackstone from Kabetogama
Forsakes his wigwam and his squaw.
    The trail he takes
    O'er frozen lakes
Through swamp and forest, slush and snow.

Red Lake sent all his braves along
With Wame Tegoose, Chief of Sabaskong,
    And from Savanne
    Came Fiery Hand,
A warrior famed in Indian song.

The plan was a bold and cruel one:

And then the Council formed a plan,
To meet together, every man
    With one accord
    To dash aboard,
And seize the *Fleetwing* as she ran.

Today in the Borderlands

Then, having captured the steamboat, the Council urged:

And when they neared Rat Portage town
Noiselessly drop the anchor down:
    And then to creep,
    In midnight deep,
And burn each dwelling to the ground.

And when the town was blazing bright
To make their exit in the night;
    Not e'en look back
    Till on the track
They flag the first train come in sight.

Just what would be the scheme after boarding the Canadian Pacific train is not revealed by the poem, but the plan was abandoned anyway, after Wake 'Em Up rose in council and poured cold water on the strategy.

The wild richness of the borderlands is best proved by the fact that Indians can still live there as of old. Wherever one travels on the border, one catches glimpses of natives in dome-shaped wigwams perched on rocky shores, from which blue-gray smoke drifts lazily up toward fleecy clouds and azure heavens. Here, where the great god Pan of the Chippewa — Nanabazhoo of their remarkable folk tales — smoked his dogwood kinnikinnick while enjoying friendly intercourse with the red men, the white man who is attuned to Nature's subtle melodies may still hear the reed pipes playing softly. For the waves still lap musically on sand beaches, rush thunderously up rocky inlets, bear millions of feathered folk on their glinting crests, cradle whole finny tribes, and echo the soughing of pines. Arbutus still scents the air in spring, wild roses brighten every crag and waterfall's edge in summer, and blue gentians rival the cloudless skies of autumn. And in winter the world is pure and bright once more, as one snowshoes between white-laden spruces, spiring heavenward.

Bibliography

A LIST OF THE MORE IMPORTANT WORKS CONSULTED IN THE
PREPARATION OF THIS BOOK

ANDERSON, PAUL. Minnesota Logging by Railroad Moves into the
Past. A manuscript in Anderson's possession. It is printed in
slightly different form in the International Falls Daily Journal,
August 19, 1947.

BELCOURT, GEORGES ANTOINE. Mon itinéraire du Lac des Deux-
Montagnes à la Rivière-Rouge. (Bulletin de la Société His-
torique de Saint-Boniface, v. 4). Montreal, [1913].

BERG, JUDGE JOHN. Reminiscences. A manuscript in the possession
of the Koochiching County Historical Society.

BIDDISON, JOSEPH. Reminiscences. A manuscript in the possession
of the Koochiching County Historical Society.

BIGSBY, DR. JOHN J. The Shoe and Canoe, or Pictures of Travel
in the Canadas. . . . London, 1850.

BLEGEN, THEODORE C. Fort St. Charles and the Northwest Angle.
In Minnesota History, v. 18, p. 231–248. September, 1937.

BROWN, ERNEST L. Diaries, 1889–1901. These manuscript diaries
are in the possession of the Minnesota Historical Society.

BURPEE, LAWRENCE J., editor. Journals and Letters of Pierre Gaultier de Varennes de La Vérendrye and His Sons. . . . (Publi-
cations of the Champlain Society, v. 16). Toronto, 1927.

——— The Search for the Western Sea: The Story of the Exploration of Northwestern America. Toronto, 1935.

CHAPIN, EARL V. Chapin's No. 1 Tourguide. . . . A Guide to
Minnesota's Border Country. Roseau, 1946.

COUES, ELLIOTT, editor. New Light on the Early History of the
Greater Northwest: The Manuscript Journals of Alexander
Henry . . . and of David Thompson . . . 1799–1814. . . .
New York, 1897. 3 v.

Rainy River Country

Cox, Ross. Adventures on the Columbia River, Including the Narrative of a Residence of Six Years on the Western Side of the Rocky Mountains. . . . Together with a Journey across the American Continent. London, 1831. 2 v.

Dean, Michael C., compiler. Flying Cloud, and One Hundred and Fifty Other Old Time Songs and Ballads. . . . Virginia, [1922].

Delafield, Major Joseph. The Unfortified Boundary: A Diary of the First Survey of the Canadian Boundary Line from St. Regis to the Lake of the Woods. Edited by Robert McElroy and Thomas Riggs. New York, 1943.

Dobie, John. A Northern Landmark Passes. In Conservation Volunteer, v. 9, p. 34. May–June, 1946.

Drummond, William Henry. The Voyageur and Other Poems. New York, 1905.

Dufferin and Ava, Hariot Georgina, Marchioness of. My Canadian Journal, 1872–78; Extracts from My Letters Home. . . . New York, 1891.

Duncan, Norman. Higgins – A Man's Christian. In Harpers' Monthly Magazine, v. 119, p. 166–179. July, 1909.

Durham, Jeremiah W. Minnesota's Last Frontier. [Minneapolis, 1925]. Reprinted from the Roseau Times.

Evans, James. Diaries. These manuscript diaries are owned by the University of Western Ontario. The Minnesota Historical Society has typewritten copies of most of them.

Faries, Hugh. See Gates, Charles M., editor.

Folwell, William W. A History of Minnesota. St. Paul, 1921–30. 4 v. Portions of volume 4 relating to the Chippewa Indians and pineland matters were especially valuable in preparing this book.

Fort Frances Times. Fort Frances, Ontario. The issues of December 10, 1925, (with the supplement to the special edition of that date) and of June 5, 1941, were of special significance for this volume.

Franchere, Gabriel. Narrative of a Voyage to the Northwest Coast of America in the Years 1811, 1812, 1813 and 1814. . . . Translated and edited by J. V. Huntington. New York, 1854.

FROBISHER, BENJAMIN and JOSEPH. Letter to Governor Ferdinand Haldimand, October 4, 1784. In Report on Canadian Archives, 1890. Edited by Douglas Brymner. Ottawa, 1891.

FRYKLUND, P. O. A Catalog of Copper from Roseau County, Minnesota. In Minnesota Archaeologist, v. 7, no. 3, p. 4–16. July, 1941.

GALE, EDWARD C. Up the Rainy Lake River. In Minnesota History, v. 24, p. 276–286. December, 1943. Reprinted from the Literary Northwest, v. 2, p. 211–218. February, 1893.

GARRY, NICHOLAS. Diary. In Transactions of the Royal Society of Canada, second series, v. 6, sec. 2, p. 73–204. Ottawa, 1900.

GATES, CHARLES M., editor. Five Fur Traders of the Northwest; Being the Narrative of Peter Pond and the Diaries of John Macdonell, Archibald N. McLeod, Hugh Faries, and Thomas Connor. Minneapolis, 1933.

GRAHAM, FREDERICK ULRIC. Notes of a Sporting Expedition in the Far West of Canada, 1847. Edited by Jane Hermione Graham. London, 1898.

GRANT, GEORGE M. Ocean to Ocean: Sandford Fleming's Expedition through Canada in 1872. Toronto, 1925.

HENRY, ALEXANDER. Travels & Adventures in Canada and the Indian Territories between the Years 1760 and 1776. Edited by James Bain. Boston, 1901.

—— See COUES, ELLIOTT, editor.

HINCKLEY, I. W. An Early History of Littlefork. Littlefork, 1942.

HIND, HENRY Y. Narrative of the Canadian Red River Exploring Expedition of 1857 and of the Assinniboine and Saskatchewan Exploring Expedition of 1858. London, 1860. 2 v.

HUDSON'S BAY COMPANY. Archives. London, England. In this enormous collection of records of the company from 1667 to date, the most valuable in preparing this book were the diaries of men in charge of Lac La Pluie District, 1793–1841; the Escabitchewan journal of 1792–93; and the reports of Lac La Pluie District, 1816–35. These include the diaries of John McKay, Donald MacPherson, Robert Logan, Roderick McKenzie, and others; and the reports of Dr. John McLoughlin,

Rainy River Country

Simon McGillivray, J. D. Cameron, and others. Permission to use these records was graciously accorded by the Governor and Committee of the Hudson's Bay Company.

HUYSCHE, G. L. The Red River Expedition. New York, 1871.

INNIS, HAROLD A. The Fur Trade in Canada: An Introduction to Canadian Economic History. New Haven, 1930.

INTERNATIONAL FALLS DAILY JOURNAL.

INTERNATIONAL FALLS ECHO. Anniversary number. January 5, 1906.

INTERNATIONAL FALLS PRESS. The historical edition of April 4, 1906, was of special value in writing this book.

INTERNATIONAL JOINT COMMISSION. Final Report . . . on the Lake of the Woods Reference. Washington, 1917.

JACOBS, PETER. Journal of the Reverend Peter Jacobs, Indian Wesleyan Missionary, from Rice Lake to the Hudson's Bay Territory, and Returning; Commencing May, 1852. . . . New York, 1857.

JAMES, JAMES ALTON. The First Scientific Exploration of Russian America and the Purchase of Alaska. Chicago, 1942. Robert Kennicott's diary and other information about him are included.

JOHNSON, HORACE. Gold Rush to the Vermilion and Rainy Lake Districts of Minnesota and Ontario in 1865 and 1894. [Duluth], 1926.

KANE, PAUL. Wanderings of an Artist among the Indians of North America from Canada . . . through the Hudson's Bay Company's Territory. . . . Toronto, 1925.

KEATING, WILLIAM H. Narrative of an Expedition to the Source of St. Peter's River, Lake Winnepeek, Lake of the Woods, &c., Performed in the Year 1823 . . . under the command of Stephen H. Long, U.S.T.E. London, 1825. 2 v.

KENNICOTT, ROBERT. See JAMES, JAMES ALTON.

KENORA, ONTARIO. Centennial Review. N.p., 1936.

KRUSE, HARVEY. Another Yuma Is Found. . . . In Minnesota Archaeologist, v. 7, no. 3, p. 21. July, 1941.

——— Three New Discoveries in America. . . . In Minnesota Archaeologist, v. 7, no. 1, p. 52–54. January, 1941.

Bibliography

LA VÉRENDRYE, PIERRE GAULTIER, SIEUR DE. See BURPEE, LAW-
RENCE J., editor.

LEVERETT, FRANK. Quaternary Geology of Minnesota and Parts
of Adjacent States. (U.S. Geological Survey. Professional Paper
no. 161). Washington, 1932.

—— Relative Length of Pleistocene Glacial and Interglacial
Stages. In Science, v. 72, p. 193–195. August, 1930.

MACDONELL, JOHN. See GATES, CHARLES M., editor.

McGILLIVRAY, DUNCAN. Some Account of the Trade Carried on
by the North West Company. In Dominion of Canada, Report
of the Public Archives for the Year 1928, p. 56–73. Ottawa,
1929.

MACKENZIE, ALEXANDER. Voyages from Montreal through the
Continent of North America to the Frozen and Pacific Oceans
in 1789 and 1793. . . . New York, 1903.

MACKENZIE, WILLIAM ROY, collector. Ballads and Sea Songs
from Nova Scotia. Cambridge, 1928. This collection includes
"The Maid of the Mountain Brow."

McLOUGHLIN, JOHN. Description of the Indians from Fort William to Lake of the Woods. A manuscript owned by the library
of McGill University, Montreal. The Minnesota Historical Society has a photostatic copy.

MANDONIAN, THE. Minneapolis, 1946–49. This is the house organ
of the Minnesota and Ontario Paper Company.

MARTIN, PAUL S., GEORGE I. QUIMBY, and DONALD COLLIER. Indians before Columbus. Chicago, [1947]. One section deals
with prehistoric Indians in Minnesota.

MINNESOTA. State Census, 1895. Manuscript schedules in the possession of the Minnesota Historical Society.

MOORE, JOHN BASSETT. History and Digest of the International
Arbitrations to Which the United States Has Been a Party.
. . . Washington, 1898. 6 v. Volume 1 contains data on the
northern Minnesota boundary dispute; volume 6 includes David Thompson's maps of canoe routes between Lake Superior
and Lake of the Woods.

MORTON, ARTHUR S. Sir George Simpson, Overseas Governor of the Hudson's Bay Company: A Pen Picture of a Man of Action. Portland, 1944.

NICHOLAS, WILLIAM H. Men, Moose, and Mink of Northwest Angle. In National Geographic Magazine, v. 92, p. 265–284. August, 1947.

NUTE, GRACE LEE, editor. Documents Relating to Northwest Missions, 1815–1827. St. Paul, 1942.

———— Hudson's Bay Company Posts in the Minnesota Country. In Minnesota History, v. 22, p. 270–289. September, 1941.

———— Lake Superior. Indianapolis, [1944].

———— The Voyageur. New York, 1931.

———— The Voyageur's Highway: Minnesota's Border Lake Land. St. Paul, 1941.

OEHLER, C. M. Time in the Timber. (Minnesota Historical Society, Forest Products History Foundation Series, Publication No. 2). St. Paul, 1948.

O'LEARY, PETER. Travels and Experiences in Canada, the Red River Territory, and the United States. London, 1875.

OWEN, DAVID DALE. Report of a Geological Survey of Wisconsin, Iowa, and Minnesota. . . . Philadelphia, 1852.

PRITCHETT, JOHN PERRY. The Red River Valley, 1811–1849: A Regional Study. New Haven, 1942.

RAINY LAKE HERALD. (Rainy Lake City.)

RAINY LAKE JOURNAL. (Rainy Lake City.)

RICHARDSON, SIR JOHN. Arctic Searching Expedition: A Journal of a Boat-Voyage through Rupert's Land and the Arctic Sea. . . . 2 v. London, 1851.

SIMPSON, SIR GEORGE. An Overland Journey Round the World, during the Years 1841 and 1842. Philadelphia, 1847.

STUNTZ, GEORGE. A letter concerning his explorations in northern Minnesota. In William F. Leggett and Frederick J. Chipman, Duluth and Environs, p. 67–70. Duluth, [1895].

TANNER, JOHN. A Narrative of the Captivity and Adventures of John Tanner (U.S. Interpreter at the Sault de Ste. Marie) during Thirty Years Residence among the Indians in the Interior of North America. Edited by Edwin James. New York, 1830.

THOMPSON, DAVID. Diaries and maps. Manuscripts owned by the Department of Public Records and Archives of the Province of Ontario at Toronto. The Minnesota Historical Society has photostatic copies of many of them.

―――― See COUES, ELLIOTT, editor.

―――― See MOORE, JOHN BASSETT.

―――― See TYRRELL, JOSEPH B., editor.

TYRRELL, JOSEPH B., editor. David Thompson's Narrative of his Explorations in Western America, 1784–1812. Toronto, 1916.

UNITED STATES. Department of the Interior. General Land Office, Letters Received. Reports and letters of special timber agents, especially those of John W. Jones, February 9, 1878; Webster Eaton, August 31, September 26, 1883; N. B. Wharton, July 7, 1888; J. S. Wallace, April 21, 1890; A. S. Stiles, February 8, 1895; and A. F. Naff, April 10, 1896. Also records of timber trespass cases in the same office. These archives are in the possession of the National Archives at Washington. Miss Lucile Kane, curator of manuscripts of the Minnesota Historical Society, generously made her notes on these archives available to the author.

VIRGINIA AND RAINY LAKE LUMBER COMPANY. Records. Typewritten copies in the possession of the Minnesota Historical Society.

WALLACE, W. STEWART, editor. Documents Relating to the North West Company. Toronto, 1934.

WESLEYAN METHODIST MISSIONARY SOCIETY. Annual Reports, 1840–1858. London. The Minnesota Historical Society has photostatic copies of most of the reports that relate to the Rainy River missions.

WHITE, TRUMBULL and KATHERINE. Through Darkest America. In Outing, v. 21, p. 3–10, 92–100, 197–203, 320–324, 396–401, 461–463. October, 1892–March, 1893.

WHITTLES, THOMAS D. The Lumberjack Sky Pilot. Chicago, 1908.

Rainy River Country

—— The Parish of the Pines; the Story of Frank Higgins, the Lumberjacks' Sky Pilot. New York, [1912].

WHITTLESEY, CHARLES. Geology and Minerals; a Report of Explorations in the Mineral Regions of Minnesota during the Years 1848, 1859, and 1864. Cleveland, 1866.

WILFORD, LLOYD A. Minnesota Archaeology, with Special Reference to the Mound Area. A manuscript doctoral dissertation in the possession of Harvard University. 1937.

—— The Prehistoric Indians of Minnesota. In Minnesota History, v. 25, p. 153–157. June, 1944.

—— The Prehistoric Indians of Minnesota: The Headwaters Lakes Aspect. In Minnesota History, v. 26, p. 312–329. December, 1945.

WINCHELL, HORACE V. Report of Observations Made during the Summer of 1887. In Geological and Natural History Survey of Minnesota, Sixteenth Annual Report, 1887, p. 395–478. St. Paul, 1888.

WINCHELL, NEWTON W. The Aborigines of Minnesota. . . . St. Paul, 1911.

YOUNG, EGERTON R. The Apostle of the North, Rev. James Evans. New York, [1899].

Index

Rainy River Country

Rainy River Country

Morris Act, *1902*, 58, 85
Morrison, Allan, 30, 31
Monsoni Indians, 6
Morrison, Michel, 63
Morrison, William, 30, 39
Mound builders, 2, 9
Mountain Iron, lumbering, 92
Muskeg Bay, Lake of the Woods, 110

NAMAKAN LAKE, steamboats, 49;
pines, 57; hoist, 93; dams, 116
Namakan Lumber Co., 59
National Pole and Treating Co., 89
Nelson Act, *1889*, 58
Nestor Falls, 109
Nett Lake Indian Reservation, 53, 110
Nett River, log drive, 123
Norman, 38, 54, 107, 108, 116
Norquist, John, 55
North West Co., 1, 29; posts, 1, 14–17, 21, 22, 38, 84, *see also* individual posts; merges with X Y Co., 18; absorbed by Hudson's Bay Co., 22, 31
Northern Construction Co., 107
Northern Lumber Co., 91
Northern Navigation Co., 86
Northern Pacific Railroad, 103
Northome, 114
Northwest Angle, 26, 41, 50, 64, 70, 108, 114; proposed road to, 46; treaty, 61; state forest, 111; steamboats to, 115
Northwest Bay, Rainy Lake, 39
Norway House, 35

O'BRIEN, WILLIAM, 92
O'Leary, Peter, 47, 48, 84
Ontario, dispute over territory, 69; industries, 115
Ontario and Minnesota Power Co., Ltd., 106
Ontario Lumber Co., 57
Ontario-Minnesota Pulp and Paper Co., Ltd., 106, 108

Orr, roads, 109
Owen, David D., 42

PALLISER, JOHN, 46
Paper mills, 89, 106, 118, 120
Parker, G. S., 85
Patricia area, logging, 120, 121
"Patty the Bird," prospector, 77
Pelan, 70
Pelland, road, 109
Pembina, posts, 22; mission, 34
Pengilly, 104
Peterson family, 64
Pickle Crow area, mining, 73
Pigeon River, 13; trade route, 5; international boundary, 27
Pine Creek, logging, 55
Pine Island State Forest, 110
Pither's Point, Rainy River, 7
Poles, 119
Pond, Peter, 15
Port Arthur, 17, 49, 75
Power plants, 116
Prince Arthur's Landing, *see* Port Arthur
Provencher, Joseph N., 23, 34
Public lands, logging, 54–58, 85; sales, 58, 62; surveys, 62, 79, 81

QUETICO PROVINCIAL PARK, 110
Quetico-Superior Council, 117

RAILROADS, 50, 52, 87; logging, 58, 59, 83, 89, 92, 93, 103–106
Rainy Lake (Lac La Pluie, Tecamamiouen), 1, 15, 34, 44; posts, 6, 10, 15–18, 21, 23, 25, 28, 29, 31, 37; Indians, 6, 15; missionaries, 22, 37; steamboats, 49, 51, 74–76, 86; log drives, 52; pines, 57; mining, 72–80; hoist, 93; camps, 96, 99; sawmills, 107; tourists, 110, 115, 122; islands, 111; power production, 116; dams, 116; roads, 122; fishing, 122; York boats, 123

Lake
Winnipeg
English River
Winnipeg River
Clay Lak
Eag
Dalles
Rat Portage
LAKE OF
THE WOODS
Lac
Plat
Whitefish
Lake
Northwest
Angle
Long Sault
Manitou Rapids
NW Co.
Ft.
Rainy River
Black
River
Big Fork River
River aux
Rapides
Red River of the North